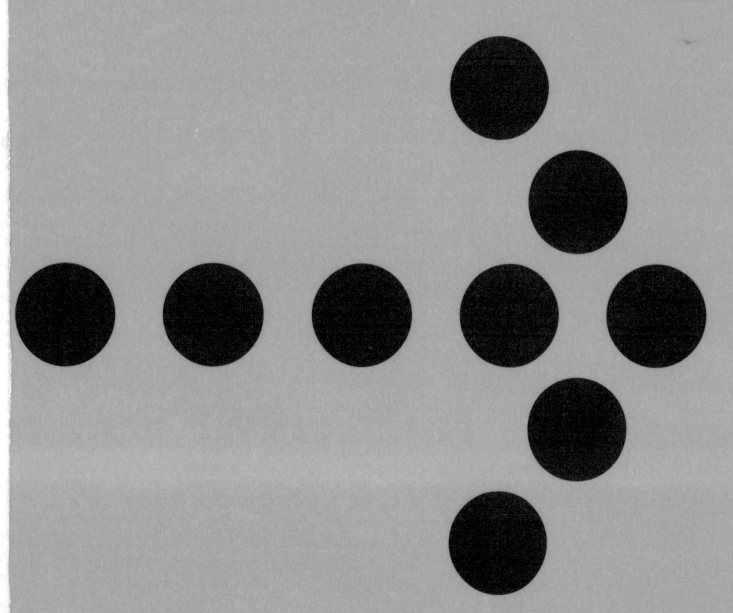

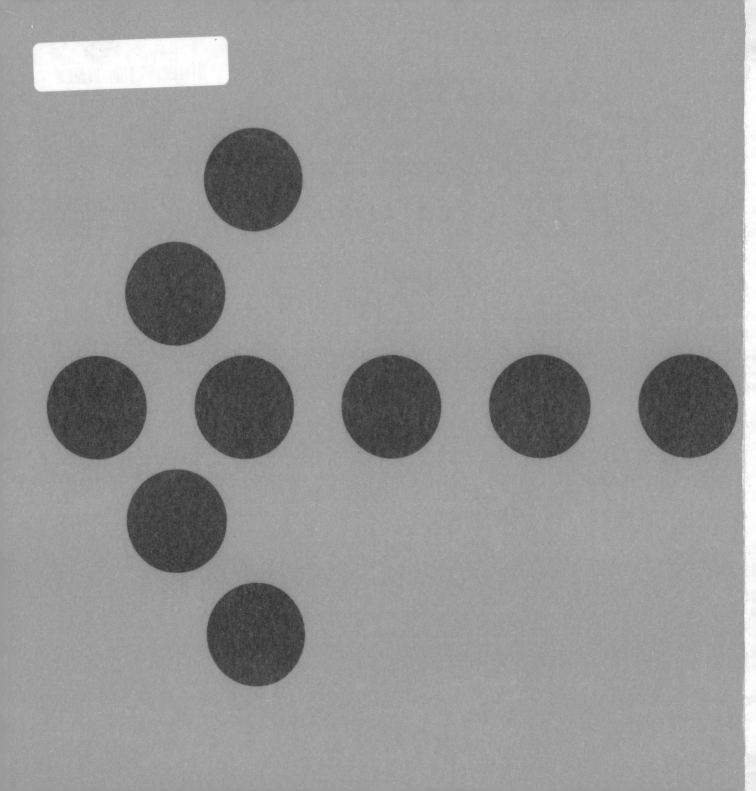

MetaDesign

Erik sm

FAY SWEET

MetaDesign

Design from the Word Up

WATSON-GUPTILL
PUBLICATIONS
New York

First published in 1999 in the United States of America
by Watson-Guptill Publications, a division of
BPI Communications, Inc.,
1515 Broadway, New York, NY 10036

Library of Congress Catalog Card Number: 99-65024

ISBN 0-8230-1212-3

This book was conceived,
designed, and produced by
THE IVY PRESS LTD
The Old Candlemakers
West Street
Lewes
East Sussex BN7 2NZ

Art Director: Peter Bridgewater
Editorial Director: Denny Hemming
Project Manager: Christine Davis
Designer: Alan Osbahr
Senior Project Editor: Rowan Davies

Originated and printed by Hong Kong Graphic, Hong Kong

Contents

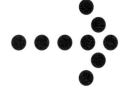

'**W**hen I first thought of looking for partners to start a design studio, my aim was very simple: I wanted to hang out with bright people, do cool work for demanding clients, and have a good time doing so. That won't quite suffice as a proper mission statement, something every company seems to have these days. Various attempts at writing down the MetaDesign mission have been made, but sometimes I think if you have to write it down, you've already lost it. We have always hired more for attitude than portfolios, and I like to think that we all have a pretty good idea what Meta is all about, even though not everybody may be able to put it into the same precise words. Let me try: At MetaDesign, we look at the big picture (often beyond the brief), and we take care of tiny detail. Our work can change a client's culture, but it also manifests itself in how well a document can be read on their computer screens. MetaDesign is about turning powerful ideas into everyday experiences. **"** Erik Spiekermann

DESIGN IS A TROUBLING WORD. It lacks precision. To most people it means something visual; but for Erik Spiekermann, design, first and foremost, is an intellectual process, "a way of tackling problems and producing elegant solutions." Although always clear and concise, Spiekermann is much more than the high priest of logic: he is witty and subversive, incisive and inspiring, cantankerous and charming. He has achieved world renown as one of our most successful typeface designers, and through his company MetaDesign has demonstrated that the most powerful and enduring graphic communication must be built on intellectual foundations.

Founded in 1979 in Berlin, MetaDesign has grown from a small studio specializing in type and graphics to a global communication design company. It is now in its third incarnation. MetaDesign phase I enjoyed a brief life from 1979 to 1983; phase II existed from 1984 to 1989, and the current Meta phase III was founded in 1990. Just as you might expect, the work includes all aspects of information design from made-to-order typefaces to corporate identities, signs, brochures, packaging, and Web sites. But at the same time, MetaDesign has been quietly reinventing

notions of design and the role of the designer. The so-called "design for design" activities, for example, form an important part of MetaDesign's work. This involves MetaDesign providing the elements, tools, and guides that will enable a company or organization to implement its own corporate identity—rather like a do-it-yourself design kit. More unusual still is the latest wave of work that digs deep into the client's world to redesign its working practices, its products, and its business plan alongside, and integrated with, involvement on the visible face of the company. It is an approach that requires enlightened clients, but MetaDesign has found that they're not in short supply.

To reflect its unusual spread of work, the Berlin office has also evolved an unusual structure. The company has become decentralized and is divided into near-autonomous teams. They perform like a series of small companies working under the Meta umbrella. Each team is named for a color and includes graphic designers, a senior designer, and a project manager. In addition to these teams, there are others specializing in 3-D design, typographic design, and consulting; there's even a psychologist who supports the teams in strategic developments. The teams are

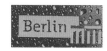

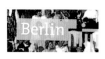

MetaDesign's work for the reunified Berlin city council (1993) exemplifies the company's "Design for Design" approach. In addition to creating the logo and initial designs for printed communications, Meta produced templates and documentation to be used by in-house designers.

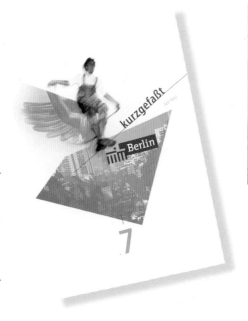

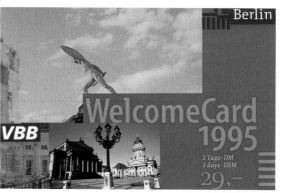

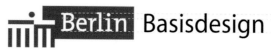

encouraged to develop their own particular strengths, but the MetaDesign culture provides the glue to bind them together. With a company of more than 200 people, it's no longer feasible, or desirable, to operate the master-and-apprentice style of working; and while Spiekermann clearly remains a key figure, his fellow partners play their own roles in running the show. Joining the German office are others in San Francisco (founded in 1992) and London (founded in 1995). The cross-fertilization of ideas and exchange of staff has been important in establishing MetaDesign's credentials in serving global businesses.

While each studio has its own distinct character, all use the intellectual discipline of design to organize information, and share the same core philosophy of a love of type and a systematic approach to projects. Because of its proximity to Silicon Valley, the San Francisco office has particular expertise in digital technology and interface design. Says partner Terry Irwin: "We are on the front line of changes being created by the Web and we're witnessing its impact on corporate culture. To survive and succeed, businesses today have to deliver better services, and they're looking to people like us to help them achieve that, using our skills in problem-solving and inventing." The London office, meanwhile, is the smallest of the trio and has a slightly more experimental feel than the others. "We're now seeing new uses for traditional design skills," says partner Tim Fendley. "We're also moving into new areas such as product development and management consultancy. Our jobs are changing so much, we'll soon need to find a new word to describe what we do."

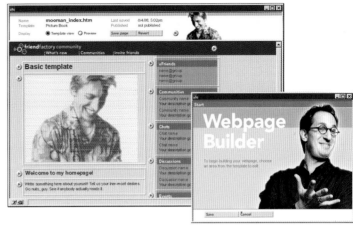

Above: Because of its proximity to Silicon Valley, the San Francisco office has particular expertise in digital technology and interface design. Shown here are two screens from Sony's Friend Factory, an online community being developed for German and British markets. At right is the home page of the MetaDesign Web site at www.metadesign.com.

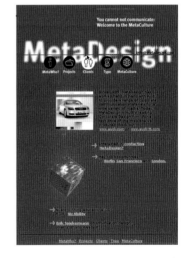

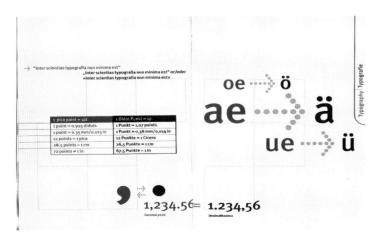

Spread from the A6 book created for delegates attending the 1996 Aspen Design Conference. Written by Erik Spiekermann and Terry Irwin and designed by the San Francisco office, the handbook cleverly plays with Anglo-American / German cultural and language differences while demonstrating the international language of good design.

Formative years

The MetaDesign success story has humble beginnings. In the monochrome world of postwar Hannover, a bright young kid with a ruffle of blond hair became fascinated by the "whoosh, bang" noise coming from a neighbor's workshop. "I'll always remember that sound: it was an old Heidelberg Platen press and it clattered and clanked from morning until night." This was how Erik Spiekermann became introduced to type. "The best thing was that they used to give me all the paper trimmings so I could draw on them. The narrow strips were ideal for cartoons."

It wasn't long before the young Erik's interest moved from the paper to the printing press itself: "I'll never forget the heat and oily smell of the Linotype setting machine." Late in the decade, the Spiekermann family moved to Bonn. "I couldn't believe my luck. Over the yard from where we lived there was another printer, the Bonn University Press. It's still there. When I was 12, I was given my first small tabletop press and a few handfuls of metal type. I used it to produce the school magazine. I did the whole lot, from setting the columns of type through to pasting up the page designs."

MetaDesign Berlin has a specialized team of 3-D designers working on projects from household products to retail environments. This bus shelter for Nordhessischer Verkehrsverbund (NVV), 1996, was conceived as a modular system that is easy to erect and highly durable.

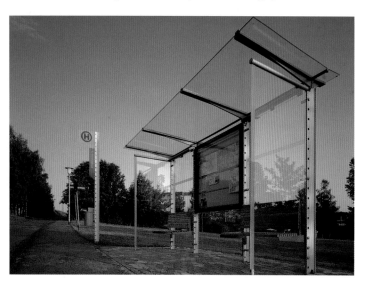

"The philosophy is to think before you act, do a little more than is required, and keep it simple."

The impassioned work of a self-confessed typomaniac, Rhyme & Reason: A Typographic Novel (first published in German in 1982, English edition 1987) was Spiekermann's plea to the design industry to recognize and maintain the best typographic standards.

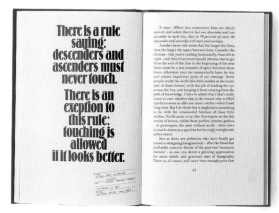

When he was 17, Spiekermann took his father's advice and moved to Berlin. "My father had been through the war and came out a pacifist. He knew I'd hate the forces, and if you lived in Berlin, you could avoid the draft for military service." Spiekermann arrived with his press and immediately set up in business. The proceeds funded him through an English and Art History course at college. These were formative years: from here were born MetaDesign's philosophy and design trademarks. "The philosophy is to think before you act, do a little more than is required, and keep it simple," explains Spiekermann. "Just like the Bauhaus designers before me, I had scarce resources and made the most of them. I knew all about expediency. I found the limitations of my materials and exploited them to the full. At the same time, the more complications you add, the longer it's going to take, and I have a bad habit of leaving everything till the last minute." Spiekermann hardly ever strays from a minimal palette of black, white, and red. Another trademark is the use of a rectangular bar running across or up the side of a page, providing a structural framework against or in which the type sits. "Now I

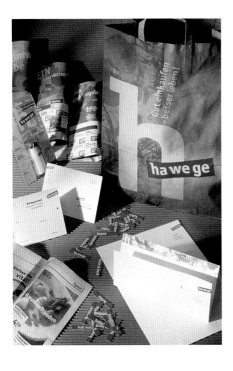

MetaDesign has worked on extensive corporate rebranding for the Tegut group of supermarkets. The cleaned-up graphics and trademark red rectangle produced in 1994 for Hawege, one of the stores in the group, give a powerful chain-store image.

"At LCP I was only a few pages ahead of my students and learned as I went along. I just about got away with it."

Move to London

In 1973 it was time to change scene again. Spiekermann had met and married an Englishwoman, Joan; they had a son and lived in an idyllic house in Berlin. "Then the landlord wanted us out. We knew we'd never find anywhere as wonderful as that house, and it seemed it was my turn to live in Joan's country, so we moved to London." Spiekermann's printing and typographic skills translated easily. He was soon working for large design companies such as Wolff Olins, Henrion Design, and Pentagram as well as type producers including Berthold and Letraset. There was also a teaching job at the London College of Printing (LCP), as well as close involvement with Filmcomposition, at the time London's leading advertising typesetters.

Once again, Spiekermann's experience contributed to the subsequent evolution of MetaDesign. British design companies gave him a taste of working for large corporate clients. The huge design studios were quite unlike anything he had experienced in Germany, where employing even a dozen graphic designers was unusual. (MetaDesign Berlin currently has about 150 staff and is the country's largest design outfit by far.) Spiekermann's

have become so fluent working within this discipline, I don't feel the need to venture outside," says Spiekermann. "Of course, the designers at Meta use a whole range of colors and are much more adventurous than I am. They must bring their own ideas to the job, but they all understand the fundamentals of economy, elegance, and legibility."

It would be easy to dismiss those early hot-metal lessons as worthless in today's digitized world. However, it is precisely Spiekermann's thorough understanding of such processes that enabled him to glide effortlessly into the print revolution of film-setting and lithography of the 1970s and 80s, and beyond into the digital 21st century. "Since I can talk the language of both printer and designer, I know where the communication breaks down. For example, to help both parties I invented a method of type specifying which was based on grid sheets for in-position setting. It cut out a whole stage of the process and reduced the possibility of error. My grid works on X-Y coordinates; it's a tectonic idea, very architectural. The fascinating thing is that this is how HTML works, so that's what builds Web pages."

Not-for-profit work is a regular feature of the MetaDesign calendar. This visual identity project was completed in 1999 for Peace Works, an initiative which every two years brings together all Nobel Peace Prize laureates to further efforts for greater world peace.

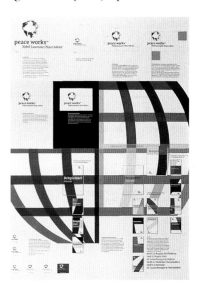

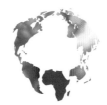

peace works™

work with type producers helped him make the leap from old to new technology—he worked with the team responsible for digitizing Berthold's entire catalog of 300 faces, bringing this classic font collection into the modern age. Also for Berthold he wrote the typographic novel *Rhyme & Reason* as a vehicle to maintain typographic standards in the face of de-skilling and the computer revolution. Almost alone in the craft-based typographic world, Spiekermann foresaw the digital explosion and spotted its creative opportunities. But far from fearing it, he embraced the new technology and ran with it. He even has the distinction of being the first designer in Germany to own an Apple computer.

The LCP experience taught Spiekermann to think on his feet. "I accepted a job to teach design—something which, in fact, I knew very little about. I was only a few pages ahead of my students and learned as I went along. I just about got away with it." The classroom provided an invaluable practice ground for public speaking. One of Spiekermann's most powerful attributes is his entertaining and enlightening lectures; he can virtually guarantee a packed-full seminar at any conference in the world.

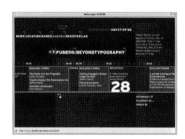

Fuse98 was a conference on experimental typography held in San Francisco in May 1998 and cosponsored by MetaDesign, Neville Brody, and FontShop International. MetaDesign developed the Fuse98 Web site as well as a stationery system, signage, and conference program.

"MetaDesign started with four of us in an old shop; we had bucketloads of energy and brilliant ideas. Most of our clients were designers—hence our slogan 'Design for Design.'"

MetaDesign is founded

The end of the 1970s saw the first incarnation of MetaDesign. "I'd heard from several German companies that they were not getting all they wanted from their British designers. For example, the British work was specified in inches, whereas German printers wanted measurements in centimeters. They came to me and a designer friend, Dieter Heil, and asked if we could help." MetaDesign was established in 1979. Heil remained in London while Spiekermann lived between London and Berlin, where he brought in another designer friend, Florian Fischer. "Our first jobs were not so much about designing as about implementing other people's designs. We had to make sure those designs worked. Functionality is still a key issue today, and testing is always a major part of any job. It's all very well creating a wonderful logo, but if it's impossible to print or takes up a massive lump of memory on your computer, it's worse than useless."

The first MetaDesign lost momentum after just four years. "We decided to split up and I was back working on my own." But not for long. "In the summer of 1983 I heard that the Deutsche Bundespost, the German post office, was asking design groups to come up with proposals for a new corporate identity. As a test job, each designer had to create a letterhead. Can you imagine the naïveté? They seriously thought that you could select the right designer for a huge job like a new corporate identity by looking at a letterhead. It was ridiculous; nevertheless, I immediately called Dieter and said let's have a go at this together." A letterhead and business card were submitted, and a summons to Bonn came days later. "It was crazy. We had virtually nothing to show, just a couple of design manuals and the post office sketches. But we went through the whole thing, pretending we were a substantial and busy company—and got the job."

Page from the MetaDesign Web site. The site reflects and reinforces the company's multidisciplinary, multinational approach to design.

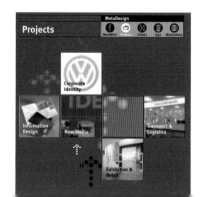

MetaDesign emerged in its second guise in 1984. The post office project was enormous, involving the redesign of every form, catalog, leaflet, and item of stationery used by the vast state-owned monolith. In 1984 the project was taken over by Sedley Place Design, who had bought Spiekermann's and Fischer's shares in MetaDesign. Spiekermann acted as consultant while running MetaDesign phase II from his office a block away; Fischer later joined Sedley Place to work on the project.

One element that was never implemented, however, was Spiekermann's design for a corporate typeface. It was conceived for maximum legibility at 7-point size, making it ideal for text-heavy forms and directories. The face began life as PT, but is known today as Meta. Released by Spiekermann in 1991, it gradually became adopted by designers worldwide as one of their favorite fonts and has become a 20th-century classic.

While Spiekermann worked as a consultant for Sedley Place, the second MetaDesign blossomed. "This is when we established the Meta reputation," recalls Spiekermann. "It started with four of us in an old shop; we had bucketloads of energy and brilliant ideas. A lot of the work was for the typographic industry and, either directly or indirectly, most of our clients were designers—hence our slogan 'Design for Design.' " Projects included elegant type specimen books for Berthold and Letraset, brochures for furniture designer Herman Miller, and an identity for the German Designers Association.

As if the workload weren't enough, Spiekermann found himself involved in yet another enterprise: setting up as the world's first digital type retailer. "This was an idea I hatched with my wife. One thing that drove designers completely nuts was being unable to buy fonts from just one source, so we set up a mail-order company called FontShop. We had no money, but we knew everyone in the industry, so we persuaded all the producers to give us copies of their fonts and then put together a catalog of 600 faces. The catalog was advertised in a handful of design magazines, and we got some good editorial coverage." The calls flooded in. Once the Berlin FontShop was established, a franchise was opened in Canada by Ed Cleary (formerly of Filmcomposition London), and then designer Neville Brody imported the idea to Britain (where it is known as FontWorks).

A logical extension to this idea was to become a publisher. "We realized that we had faces like Meta which were sitting around doing nothing, and knew dozens of other type designers who had work unreleased, so we created FontShop International as a publishing label for them." Then came a type division called FontFonts, which now boasts more than 1,200 faces. "We had the market to ourselves and were successful because we were credible. Designers knew that if we said a font worked, it did."

As the fonts rolled out, the work continued to roll in, but it was draining and allowed little time for a home life. Inevitably the pressure took its toll on personal relationships, and the Spiekermanns' marriage foundered. "I was working like crazy, my wife and son moved out, and I realized something was dreadfully wrong. Either I had to give up design altogether or run the business professionally. This time I resolved to do it properly." This was 1989, an unforgettable year in the history of Germany, Berlin, and MetaDesign. The country was reunified, it was clear that Berlin had to be stitched back together as a capital city, and the latest metamorphosis of MetaDesign was under way.

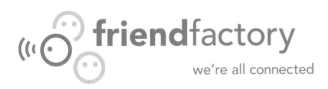

Identity for the online community Sony Friend Factory, developed by the San Francisco office.

"We wanted to prove that it was possible to work on large corporate design projects and maintain really intelligent, high-quality design solutions."

A new beginning

MetaDesign phase III opened on January 1, 1990. "This time there were three partners: my old friend Uli Mayer, the art director; Hans Christian Krüger, the business manager; and me, the design director." After a difficult start in offices at Potsdamer Platz (where all the computers were stolen), premises were found in an old factory in the southeast of the city. A prepress company was bought to guarantee quality control in repro work. "The MetaDesign focus was adjusted. We kept all the core values of designing 'from the word up' and producing really excellent type work, but this time we were aiming to build. We wanted to prove that it was possible to work on large corporate design projects and maintain really intelligent, high-quality design solutions."

Every major step in MetaDesign's history, it seems, has been marked by securing a huge project. This one was to be a commission by the Berlin Transportation Authority (BVG). With reunification came the urgent need to pull together Berlin's two public transportation systems. This meant not just fully integrated maps, but also timetables for trains, subways, trams, buses, and ferries. "The new subway and suburban train map was particularly important as an icon of the united Berlin," says Spiekermann. "It showed the city as two equal halves, and right across the middle was a graphic bridgelike structure made with half a dozen U-Bahn lines. For the first time since the war, Berliners saw the city as a whole." This job, perhaps above all others, embodies Spiekermann's reasons for becoming a designer: he has always been driven by a deep desire to make the world more accessible through the best information design, to improve communication, and to change things for the public good. Such beliefs are held by MetaDesign staff around the world.

The company grew rapidly through the 1990s. The opening of the San Francisco office (a partnership between MetaDesign Berlin and U.S. principals Bill Hill and Terry Irwin) was followed by the founding of MetaDesign London (in collaboration with principals Tim Fendley and Robin Richmond, formerly Union Design). In Berlin, meanwhile, MetaDesign had a big break when it was approached by VW and Audi, massive clients with enlightened views about the role and scope of design in the making and marketing of brands. "The initial job took six months, but we've been working with them for over five years; we now have a dedicated team of over 40 people who work solely on those accounts." With clients of this caliber, MetaDesign came of age and metamorphosed from a studio into a business.

The new grown-up MetaDesign in Berlin embraces its system of teams: Audi is in the hands of the Red team, Silver handles VW, and then there are Yellow, White, Orange, and Multicolored working on a mixture of other projects. Small experimental projects continue to find their way into the office, but the consultancy is now best known for its work with large clients on big corporate identity jobs. Whether in Berlin, San Francisco, or London, the challenges are new and enormous: how to deliver a global message and the best possible customer service worldwide, how to maximize the use of the Internet and digital technology, how to organize and make sense of vast quantities of information. But no matter how large the task, the MetaDesign approach remains the same: it is a quest to create extra value for the client via an intelligent and intellectual solution.

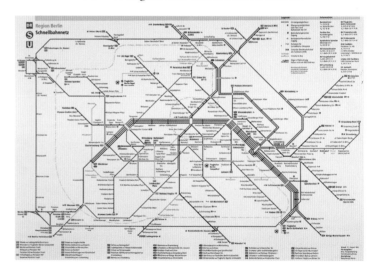

The ultimate expression of good information design. Despite its complexity, the new Berlin public transportation map succeeds in being crisp, clear, and logical.

"The new underground map was an icon of the united Berlin. For the first time since the war, Berliners saw the city as a whole."

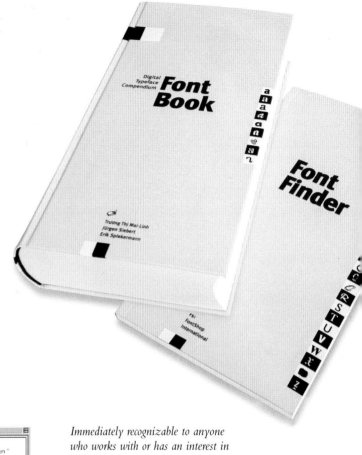

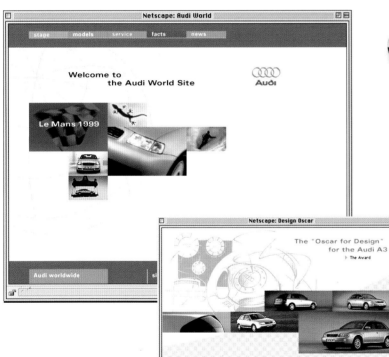

Immediately recognizable to anyone who works with or has an interest in typography, the distinctive FontBook and FontFinder are packed with type samples and font families. Erik Spiekermann coproduces these typographic bibles through his work with FontShop International.

In its work for Audi, MetaDesign has developed different Web sites to respond to different needs. The World Site is an adventure in brand experience, while the Market Site offers more practical and detailed information about the Audi product line.

MetaDesign

"THERE IS JUST one rule in successful type design," says Erik Spiekermann. "If you want a face to work and to last, it needs to fulfill a purpose. A design must have intellectual rigor, and work hard. Look at the classics: Times Roman, Franklin Gothic, Century School-book—they were all designed for newspapers or magazines, and they're all standards today. In the same way DIN [Deutsche Industrie Norm] is a German signage face that's become a world classic; and Letter Gothic, designed in the 1960s for IBM typewriters, can be seen everywhere now."

Spiekermann has added more than his fair share to those classics. There's ITC Officina, designed for maximum legibility in laser print-ers; FF Info, a signage information face first used at Düsseldorf Airport; and FF Meta, his smash hit, a slightly quirky design originated for the German post office. "Meta was deliberately created to be the complete antithesis of Helvetica," Spiekermann recalls. "Until 10 or 15 years ago, Helvetica was the ubiquitous German corporation typeface: everyone used it, and I couldn't understand why. It's so boring and bland—that's how it was designed. FF Meta was conceived for use on the post-office forms

FF INFO
Typeface design, 1996

Developed as a signage face for Düsseldorf airport, FF Info provides maximum legibility at compact sizes.

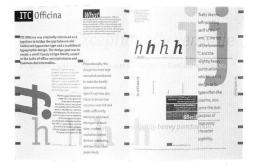

ITC OFFICINA
Typeface design, 1988/90

ITC Officina on the page: a spread from type magazine *U&lc* (top) and specimen brochure designed by Erik Spiekermann and Erik van Blokland.

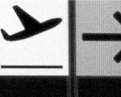

BDH
abcdeghil
mnoprstu
145

Deutsche Bundespost

Dorothea geht mit Dorothea geht mit Dorothea geht mit Dorothea geht mit
Hammer und Degen Hammer und Degen Hammer und Degen Hammer und Degen
Dorothea geht mit Dorothea geht mit Dorothea geht mit Dorothea geht mit
Hammer und Degen Hammer und Degen Hammer und Degen Hammer und Degen

24

abcdefghijklmnopqrst
uvwxyzßABCDEFGHIJKL
MNOPRSTUVWXYZ(/·.;‒
12345677890&

abcdefghijklmnopqrst
uvwxyzßABCDEFGHIJKL
MNOPRSTUVWXYZ(/·.;
12345677890&

abcdefghijklmnopqrst
uvwxyzßABCDEFGHIJKL
MNOPRSTUVWXYZ(/·.;‒
12345677890&

In February 1985 work started on what was to become the typeface Meta. It was intended for use as part of a comprehensive corporate design program for the German post office, which had been employing a spectrum of different faces. Before the new typeface was accepted, however, the entire design project was canceled. Spiekermann continued its development and launched it himself in 1991.

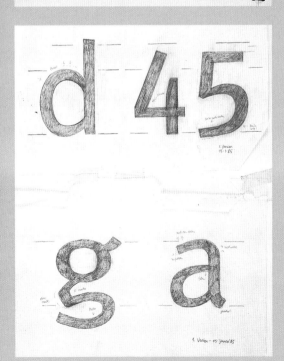

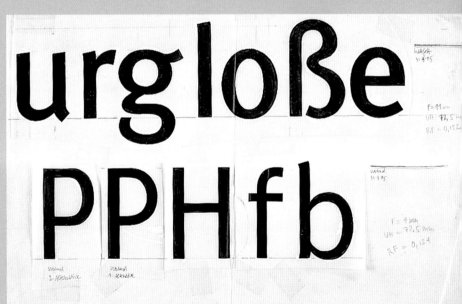

MetaPlus Book   MetaPlus Bold

MetaPlus Book Roman

abcdefghijklmnop
qrstuvwxyz
ABCDEFGHIJKLMN
OPQRSTUVWXYZ
1234567890
ä å á à â ã æ ç ë é è ê
ı ï í ì î ñ ö ó ò ô õ ø œ
ü ú ù û ÿ ß ff fi fl ffi ffl
Ä Å Á À Â Ã Æ Ç Ë É È
Ê Ï Í Ì Î Ñ Ö Ó Ò Ô Õ
Œ Ü Ú Ù Û Ÿ
¢ £ $ § & % ® © ™ Ⓜ
. … , ! ¡ ? ¿ : ; „ "" ' ' "
» « ‹ ‐ ‐ — _ ···‣ ↯‣ ·
' ( ) [ ] { } + / / \ | † ‡ °
ª º • ¶ ≠ ∞ ± ≤ ≥ ¥ µ ∂
Σ Π π ∫ Ω * ¬ √ ƒ ∆ ˆ ˜

MetaPlus Bold Roman

**abcdefghijklmnop
qrstuvwxyz
ABCDEFGHIJKLMN
OPQRSTUVWXYZ
1234567890
ä å á à â ã æ ç ë é è ê
ı ï í ì î ñ ö ó ò ô õ ø œ
ü ú ù û ÿ ß ff fi fl ffi ffl
Ä Å Á À Â Ã Æ Ç Ë É È
Ê Ï Í Ì Î Ñ Ö Ó Ò Ô Õ
Œ Ü Ú Ù Û Ÿ
¢ £ $ § & % ® © ™ Ⓜ
. … , ! ¡ ? ¿ : ; „ "" ' ' "
» « ‹ ‐ ‐ — _ ···‣ ↯‣ ·
' ( ) [ ] { } + / / \ | † ‡ °
ª º • ¶ ≠ ∞ ± ≤ ≥ ¥ µ ∂
Σ Π π ∫ Ω * ¬ √ ƒ ∆ ˆ ˜**

MetaPlus Book Caps

ABCDEFGHIJKLMNO
PQRSTUVWXYZ
ABCDEFGHIJKLMN
OPQRSTUVWXYZ
1234567890 ss

MetaPlus Bold Caps

**ABCDEFGHIJKLMN
PQRSTUVWXYZ
ABCDEFGHIJKLMN
OPQRSTUVWXYZ
1234567890 ss**

MetaPlus Book Italic

MetaPlus Book Caps Italic

MetaPlus Bold Italic

MetaPlus Bold Caps Italic

and catalogs, so it had to work on bad paper with poor quality printing at small sizes. The concept was based on research and observation. I'd found around 20 faces used in that way which nearly worked, so I took the best bits from them and made Meta." Although for internal reasons the face was never implemented by the post office, when Spiekermann later released it himself, it was adopted wholeheart-edly by the international design community. Its success has of course delighted the designer, but he is sometimes bemused by its application. "I've seen it at enormous sizes where it looks peculiar because all the quirks really show up. There were devices that we added to make the eye flow at 7 point, which look inexplicable at 24 point. The face was never finished, but I like that; it isn't too cleaned up."

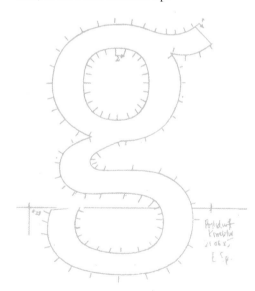

FF META
Typeface design, 1987

Exaggerated pseudo-serifs and generous curves help enhance Meta's legibility at small type sizes.

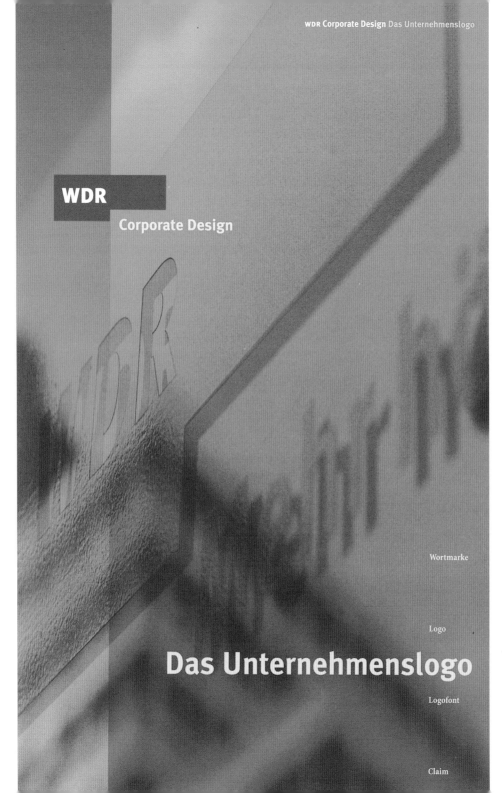

WDR

Corporate Design

Wortmarke

Logo

Das Unternehmenslogo

Logofont

Claim

W D R
Corporate identity
brochure, 1994

**MetaDesign has
produced a design
manual, logo, and
on-screen graphics
for the German
television company
WDR. MetaPlus
(shown opposite)
is one of WDR's
corporate fonts.**

Spiekermann is regularly exasperated by the numbers of badly designed typefaces he sees today, and by the general lack of understanding in how faces should be used. "You design an appropriate face by starting with questions: What is it meant to do? What is it meant to look and feel like? A typeface should provide a clear, rational, thoughtful solution underpinned by logic. Design is an intellectual activity before it is a visual one." Ever the polemicist, Spiekermann has written widely on type and typography, always with his characteristic wit and insight. His books include the classic *Rhyme & Reason: A Typographic Novel*, published in English in 1987 (originally published in German in 1982), and *Stop Stealing Sheep*, published in 1993 and cowritten with E. M. Ginger.

Despite the setbacks, Spiekermann remains optimistic about the future of his craft. "During the past decade most people have become aware of what a font is. They have them on their computers and can play around with different effects. At the same time, clients have become very brand-conscious and know that if they have their own literature they could also have their own face. It doesn't cost much, but it's worth a fortune in its impact." To demonstrate how that impact can be made, MetaDesign created one of its most innovative faces ever for the arts festival Glasgow 1999: UK City of Architecture and Design (see page 52). The punchy, muscular, and highly individual typeface was the result of examining the very concept of language itself.

FOLHA
Typeface design, 1995

This font was specially designed by MetaDesign's Director of Typographic Development, Lucas de Groot, for the newspaper *Folha de São Paulo*. For MetaDesign, a made-to-order typeface is one of the key components of a corporate identity.

ABCDEFGHIJKLMNOPQRST
UVWXYZabcdefghijklmno
pqrstuvwxyz0123456789 01
23456789:;?!ß$$&¢£§fifl

GLASGOW 1999
Typeface design, 1998

Urban, gritty, and finely engineered, this face was designed to represent Glasgow in 1999 as the UK City of Architecture and Design.

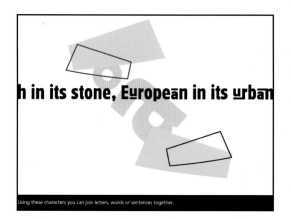

h in its stone, European in its urban

Using these characters you can join letters, words or sentences together.

āaₐAbb̲BBcc̲c̄Cdd̲doDeé̲eEfffFgḡgoGhh̲HH
iingljatinJkk̲andKll̲Lmm̲mMMnññ̲n̲Noo̲ōOpp̲
oPqq̄QQrr̲toRss̲s̄StttTuüUvv̲Vww̲w̄WxxX
youyesYzz̄Z1!!2?̄th@33̲£fﬂ44̲$ﬁ55%ﬃ
6σf№^7¶iit&88̲st*99̲9̄(00̲no).,/¿?'»«''\
ÑÉã̃fﬂÅåçæÉÑœŒõéî①❶⊛⊕⊙⊕⊕⊖⊗

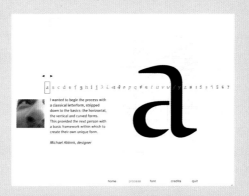

The creative minds at MetaDesign continue to push the boundaries of type design. These grabs are from CrankCall, an eccentric font produced by designers from the San Francisco office and issued as a holiday CD-ROM and downloadable font. Starting from the letter A, the alphabet was passed "Chinese whispers"-style from designer to designer, each of whom devised a new letter based on its predecessor.

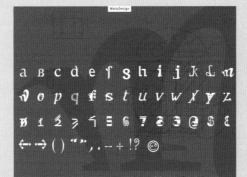

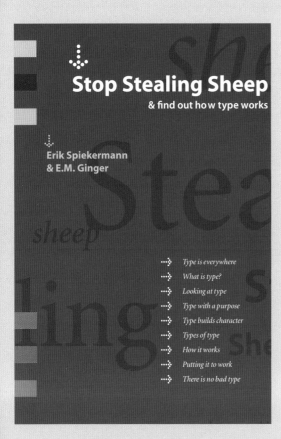

Stop Stealing Sheep
& find out how type works

Erik Spiekermann
& E.M. Ginger

STOP STEALING SHEEP
Cover and spread, 1993

Spiekermann's sequel to *Rhyme & Reason* takes its title from American type designer Frederic Goudy, who once said: "Anyone who would letterspace lowercase letters would steal sheep."

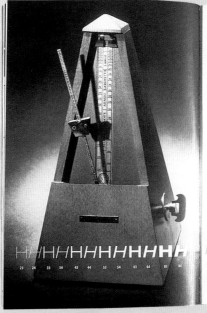

AS AN EXERCISE IN PURE information design, MetaDesign's work for the Berlin Transportation Authority, BVG, is hard to beat. The designs have striking clarity and have acted as a powerful force not only in unifying the city, but also in bestowing upon it the dignity of a capital. This complex and long-running project typifies MetaDesign's skill at organizing complex information and underlines its belief that good-quality design in the public realm can help improve the quality of urban life.

The relationship with BVG began in 1987 when MetaDesign was commissioned to put together a presentation showing how new signs and timetables could create a coherent corporate design. If it hadn't been for the events of November 1989, that presentation might never have been picked up again. As it was, BVG remembered MetaDesign.

With the fall of the Berlin Wall came the urgent need to create a semblance of normality in the reunited city. Somehow life had to go on; people still had to travel and work as they came to terms with the massive changes wrought on their lives. One of the first tangible symbols of reunification was the city's new train and underground map. This was a masterpiece of graphic engineering, bringing together on one plane the many U-Bahn, S-Bahn, and regional rail lines that serve the city and which

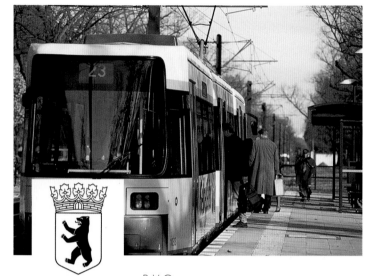

BVG
Signage and corporate design, from 1991

Unlike the old system, the new signage (below left) is highly conspicuous and helps travelers to instantly find their bearings. The bold corporate identity, applied to trains, buses, and stations, radiates modernity and efficiency.

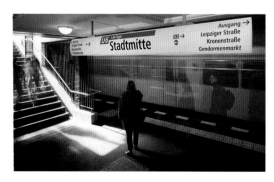

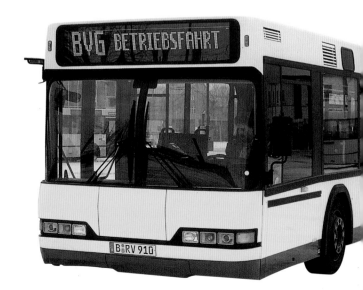

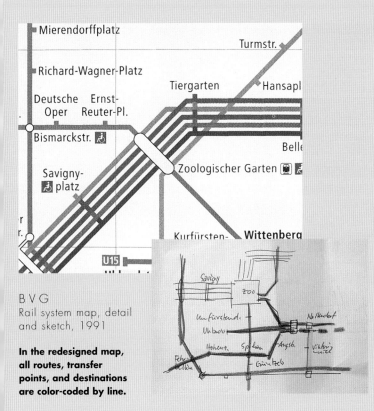

BVG
Rail system map, detail
and sketch, 1991

**In the redesigned map,
all routes, transfer
points, and destinations
are color-coded by line.**

BVG
Underground station
signage, 1991

**The signage was conceived as
a modular system. Elements
such as the line number, exit
sign, and directions to bus
stops are always in the same
position, thus aiding legibility.**

together make one of the world's most complex
commuter rail networks. The map bears a family
resemblance to the classic London Underground
map by Henry Beck. It was made under very
difficult circumstances. "Almost every month
we had to make changes, as stations in the east
reopened and lines were brought back into
use,"explains Erik Spiekermann. "But the core
of the design never changed: we kept the
'bridge' of lines spanning the center as a visual
declaration of east/west unity." Alongside
work on the map, MetaDesign was involved in
redesigning timetables for buses, subways, and
trams. These publications are so rational and
clear that they have set new standards in organizing complex and intricate information.

So successful was this early work that BVG
asked MetaDesign to follow it up with a full
corporate identity and signage system. Forming
the basis of the corporate design is the use of
the brightest possible yellow. This features in all
stationery, signage, and vehicle identities. In fact,
the simplification of the color scheme has saved
the authority a small fortune. "Before our ratio-
nalization, the manufacturers of buses and trains
would specify their own interior color schemes
and materials, but we wanted to turn this
around," explains Bruno Schmidt of the Berlin
office. "We said that if BVG were to continue
placing orders, the new colors would have to
be used. This is currently saving the authority
more than eight million deutsche marks a
year—more than our fee over five years."

U10 ▶Richtungstr. ☏ | **Ausgang** →
Musterplatz
Zufalldamm
Richard-Muster-Str.
Beispielamt

Large savings were also made possible with the introduction of a new modular signage system for the U-Bahn. MetaDesign's 3-D designers developed signs that were made of fewer elements than before, and which could be clipped together easily and then installed by just one worker. Once again, the signage itself is outstandingly clear and rational. The Frutiger-based typeface was designed specifically for the purpose. It has special versions to work under different lighting and contrast conditions as well as hundreds of arrows, pictograms, and service logos. It is now commercially available, as FF Transit, and has already been adopted by a score of other transit systems in Germany. It has also been used for new street signs in Chicago.

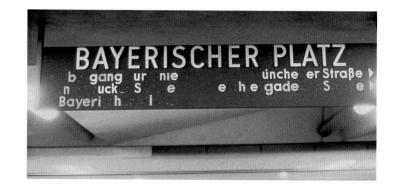

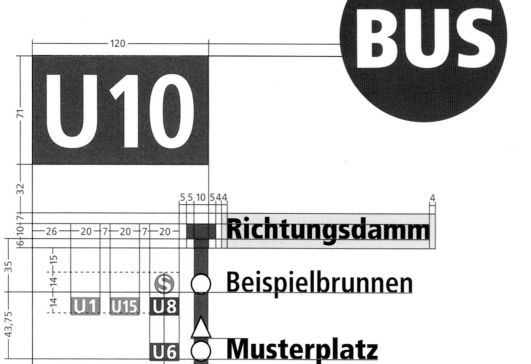

BVG
Signage design, 1991

An example from Bayerischer Platz demonstrates the sad state of the old signage, where missing letters made orientation almost impossible. MetaDesign's systematic approach includes full details of how the information elements should be displayed in relation to one another. Such consistency is of vital importance in achieving clarity.

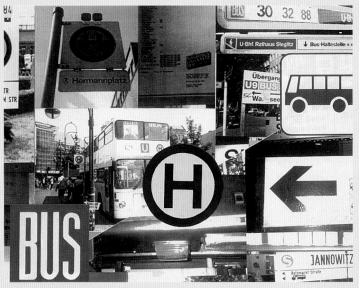

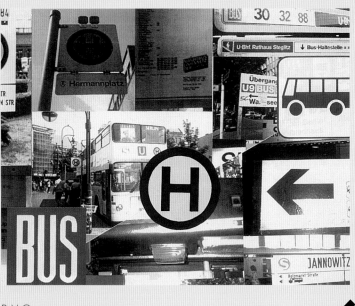

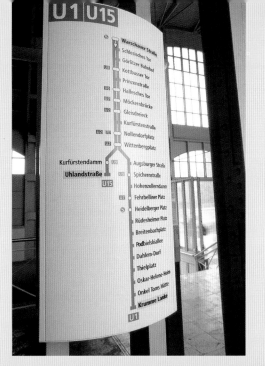

BVG
Signs and rail vehicle prototype, 1991

Before MetaDesign was called in by BVG in the late 1980s, the city's conflicting signage created visual chaos on the streets. The neat logic of the new signs is highly reassuring; the color scheme is now being extended to the interiors of buses and trains.

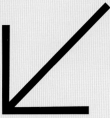

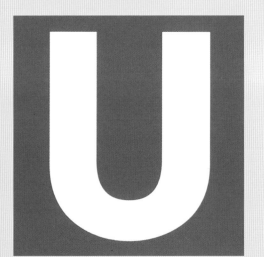

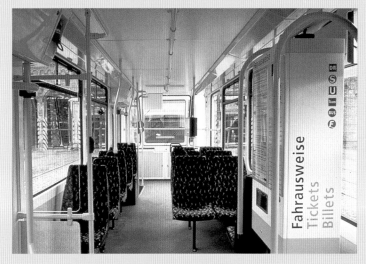

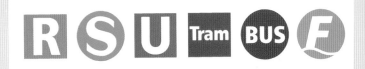

VizAbility™

VIZABILITY
Interactive learning package, 1993

Developed by scientist Christina Hooper Woolsey and MetaDesign San Francisco, this multimedia package aims to help students improve their visual skills.

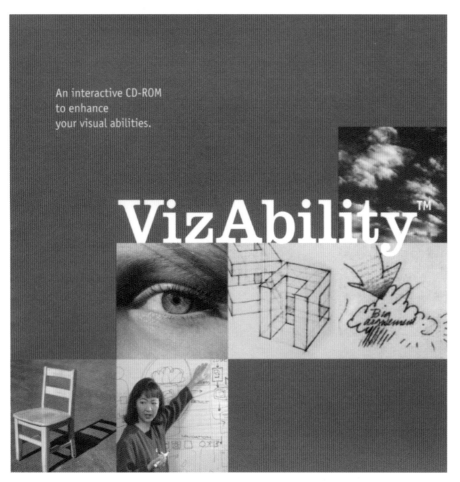

VizAbility

THIS GROUNDBREAKING CD-ROM was literally an eye-opener. In the words of partner Bill Hill: "It was really about helping people to see, giving them the confidence to trust their instincts, to understand visual language and to develop their visual sense."

The project was commissioned from Meta-Design San Francisco by educational book publisher PWS Publishing of Boston, which owned the rights to a seminal 1970s book called *Experiences in Visual Thinking* by Professor Bob McKim. Says Hill: "I knew about this book because McKim was based at Stanford University while I was there. It made fascinating reading for any student involved in the visual arts, although it had actually been written for engineers. Its basic premise was that engineers tended to focus so hard on the problem in front of them that they missed the bigger picture. This stunted their ability to solve problems creatively. The publisher saw that students' visual education and skills still could be improved and decided to republish the book, this time adding an interactive CD-ROM."

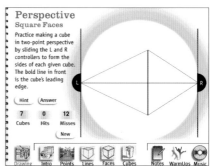

While Professor McKim endorsed the work, he didn't take an active part in the project. However, it did attract another visionary, the scientist Christina Hooper Woolsey, who had worked for Apple and at the Massachusetts Institute of Technology. She became one of the key consultants. "We built the program around a journey through six chapters, from explaining the culture of design to the much more free-form final chapter on imagining and invention," explains Hill. "There are games, puzzles, and lots of 3-D exercises. We used music, Quicktime movies, and graphics to encourage students to draw, understand spatial relationships, and even construct their own multimedia story. There are more than 60 hours of interactivity, which was considered pretty astounding in the early 1990s. In fact, the work is just as effective and pertinent today as it was then."

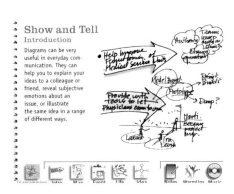

Show and Tell
Introduction

Diagrams can be very useful in everyday communication. They can help you to explain your ideas to a colleague or friend, reveal subjective emotions about an issue, or illustrate the same idea in a range of different ways.

Prototyping
Introduction

Building a prototype allows you to explore materials and refine ideas in a concrete manner. Prototypes can be quick, sketchy mock-ups or elaborately designed models. Click to see some examples.

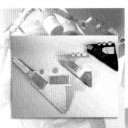

Public Space
Visit

Click on the image to view the interior of the Exploratorium. Its spacious environment and interactive exhibits create an atmosphere of informality that encourages visitors to experiment.

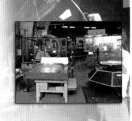

VIZABILITY
Interactive learning package, 1993

Through a program of six chapters, students are encouraged to build self-confidence in visual and practical skills. The teaching pack contains CD-ROM, step-by-step manual, and sketchbook.

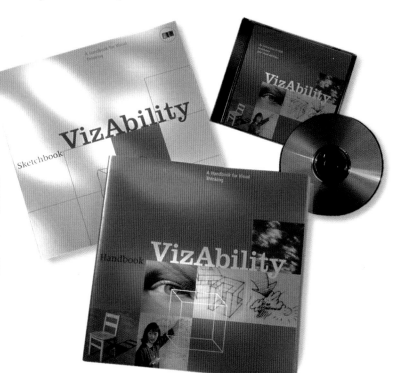

Audi

AT THE END OF 1994, the globally famous car manufacturer Audi decided to approach MetaDesign Berlin for help. The brand needed a fillip: the previous year Audi had shown losses of DM89 million. MetaDesign has since worked for a number of makers including VW, Skoda, and Lamborghini, but Audi (owned by the VW group) was their first taste of this highly competitive market.

Although the Audi line stood at the premium end of the car market, its branding was weak. A brief was developed to boost its profile and bring consistency to all its communications. "Our job was to deliver order out of the confusion," says partner Charly Frech. "Audi was operating with at least three logos in four different colors. We explained that the corporate identity and the values communicated by the company had to be the same through every aspect of design—from advertising in local papers through to brochures, showrooms, and the Web site. Everything had to support the brand concept of quality and consistency."

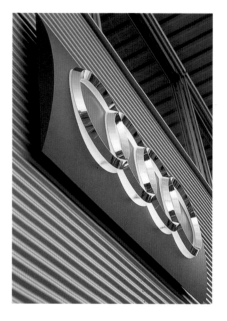

AUDI
Web sites and redrawn logo, from 1994

The four linked rings are central to Audi's corporate design. In its wide-ranging work for the company, MetaDesign has focused on consistency and clarity in promoting the premium brand image.

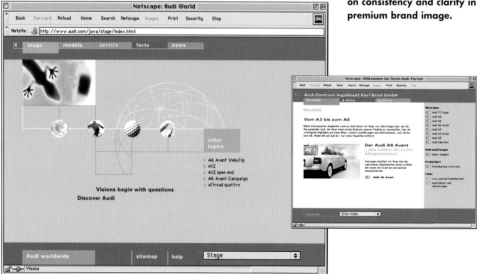

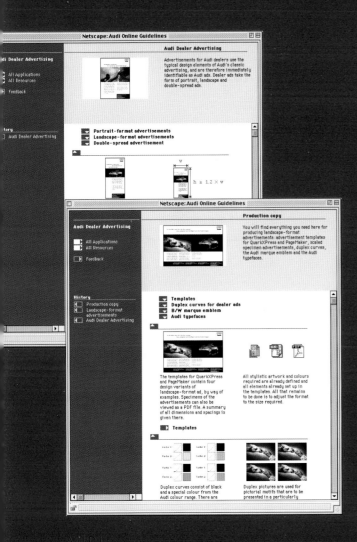

In MetaDesign's Berlin office, the Red team was established to work solely with Audi. Early improvements were made to fine-tune the famous four-ring logo, which at the time would work only at high resolution: it required too much memory to be printed on ordinary laser printers. MetaDesign reengineered the Audi logo, reducing it from several megabytes to a few kilobytes.

Digital technology has featured large in the latest chapter of the Audi story. MetaDesign saw this as a means to help the company achieve its goal of delivering a single marketing message around the world. One of the most impressive applications has been the development of an online style guide. MetaDesign has established a digital database that contains the latest logos, typeface, advertising templates, layout guidelines, and so on, and which also includes interactive design tutorials. The database is aimed at Audi's 5,000 importers, retailers, marketing companies, and advertising agencies worldwide. Using a password, they log onto the server and can download whichever elements they need to put together marketing and publicity material. There's even help given to dealers who want to construct their own Web sites: the service offers ready-prepared content and plenty of screen templates. The database replaces the more usual design manuals and CD-ROMs; it is far cheaper to maintain and can be updated in seconds. To create the database, MetaDesign developed its own dedicated software system called ERA (element, rules, application).

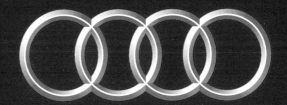

There have also been some exciting adventures in Web site design. Audi has both a German and an international site, as well as a freestanding site for the new Audi TT sports car. Here Audi and MetaDesign scored a first: the model was actually launched on the Web through a clever "teaser" site, long before it made its appearance in showrooms.

While much of the design work is digital, paper-based design manuals still have a role. One of the most recent and most unusual is for dealership architecture. Through this brochure Audi is able to pass to its retailers details of how to design and build new showrooms. It also includes (on a CD-ROM) full-scale architectural drawings with technical specifications for elements such as the roof structure, along with guidelines for signs and other details. While MetaDesign has been working with Audi, the brand has achieved a significant turnaround, and surveys have revealed greater public brand awareness. The company's fortunes have changed dramatically: the 1993 deficit had by 1996 been transformed into a DM177 million profit, which has continued to grow healthily in subsequent years.

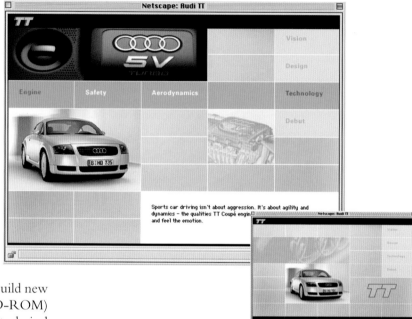

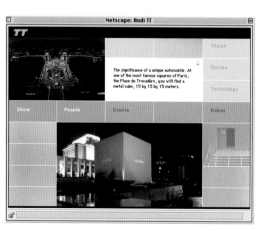

AUDI
Web site pages, 1998

In a marketing first, Audi previewed the sporty TT model on the Web before it was seen anywhere else. In the countdown to the official launch date, the teaser site revealed different aspects of the TT each day.

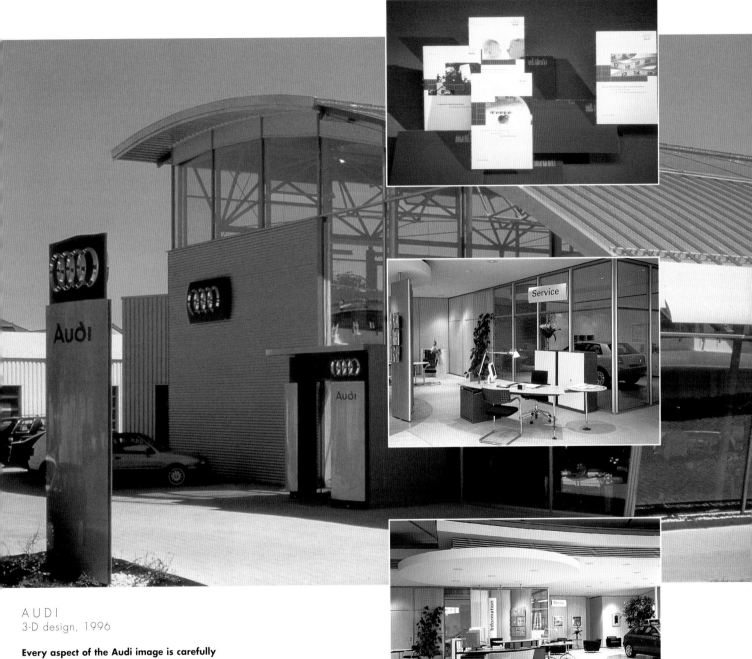

AUDI
3-D design, 1996

Every aspect of the Audi image is carefully protected, and all environments must conform to the company's exacting standards. MetaDesign has produced a brochure for retailers planning to redesign their showrooms.

AFTER YEARS OF growth and acquisitions, the pharmaceutical company Boehringer Ingelheim had amassed a family of more than 160 brands worldwide, each one retaining its old identity. It approached Meta-Design Berlin for help in drawing together this disparate collection of estranged relatives.

"We compiled a sheet of all the various brands, and it was complete chaos," says Uli Mayer, the partner in charge of the project. "There was nothing to unite them visually at all. Our approach was to bring cohesion and develop a corporate identity that could be used throughout the product line, that would proclaim the brand, and that could bring consistency to corporate stationery and packaging."

A simple and elegant logo was devised by redrawing the historical image of a roofed tower in a circle, with the company name running horizontally to the right. When used alongside brands, the company name is reduced in size and placed above the brand. A new typeface, BI Antiqua, was drawn for the purpose.

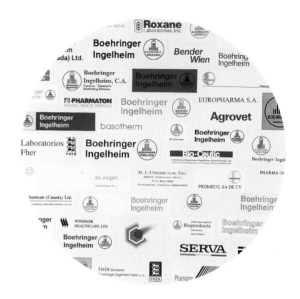

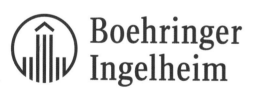

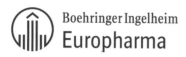

BOEHRINGER INGELHEIM
Logo design, 1995

The new corporate design had to provide a family identity for Boehringer's 160 subsidiaries, shown above in their old guises. The identity marks a new phase for the pharmaceutical company, which has made a strategic decision to sharpen the focus of its research and development activities and to streamline its management structure. The new logo can be adapted for both parent and subsidiary companies (left).

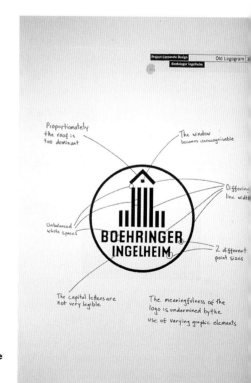

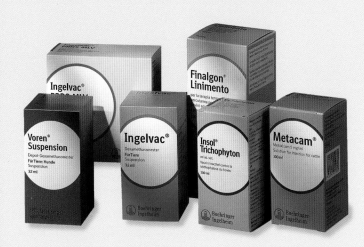

Work on unifying the packaging design was crucial to improving the branding. Here MetaDesign designed a different typeface, BI Sans, which was conceived to provide high degrees of legibility even when used at the very small point size often needed for the folded leaflets found inside packaging. Special software was even written to design the packaging automatically. "The information on packs containing medicines is carefully controlled by legislation," says Mayer. "Because the parameters are so strict there's not a great deal for a designer to do, so we investigated the possibilities of automation. A series of templates was devised for the different pack sizes, leaving operators to key in a few words. The software then composes the necessary information for that pack." Since each country has slightly different legislation, this software was customized for each market.

BOEHRINGER INGELHEIM
Corporate design, 1998

As part of its ongoing involvement with Boehringer, MetaDesign has worked on the group's corporate design manuals. The color coding is simple: red denotes the introductory brochure, yellow contains the design guidelines, and green the production guidelines.

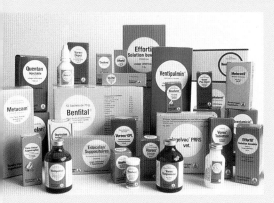

BOEHRINGER INGELHEIM
Packaging design, from 1995

In the past Boehringer Ingelheim suffered from poor branding. In this packaging for a subsidiary company, Vetmedica, it is almost impossible to detect a relationship with the parent company. The new packaging (top) is simple, appropriate, and distinctive.

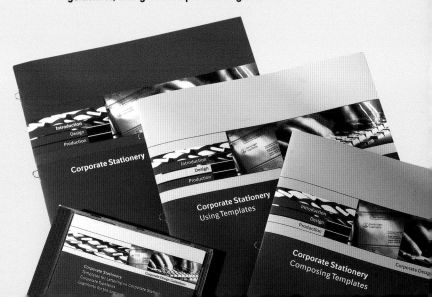

THE DÜSSELDORF AIRPORT tragedy of April 1996 left 18 people dead and more than 150 injured. An accidental fire produced dense toxic fumes, which entered the air-conditioning system and were spread around the main terminal building in minutes; trapped passengers were asphyxiated. The airport reopened after just a few days, but, with the terminal out of action, makeshift operations had to be set up in hangars and tents. "It was complete chaos; no one knew where to go. Temporary signs sprang up everywhere, and routes changed all the time, which made it impossible to get around—both for passengers and staff," recalls Bruno Schmidt of the Berlin office. "The airport authorities knew it was vital to reassure passengers that everything was being handled efficiently; they also had to keep the airlines happy and to make sure that flights were

on time. Most urgent of all, the vacation season loomed, and within six weeks passenger traffic was set to soar from 20,000 people per day to 70,000. If only half a percent of those people lost their way, there would be utter chaos."

MetaDesign knew the job would be tough, but accepted the challenge. "With one condition," adds Schmidt. "We insisted that the airport provide two senior decision-makers 24 hours a day and seven days a week to answer any questions from the designers and thus keep the process moving." A team of eight designers from the Berlin and London offices was established in one of the airport hangars. They began work by mapping out the entire site and its existing signage. The system was analyzed, and about half of the signs were found to be unhelpful or to serve no purpose. Positioning for new signs was added to the map, based on

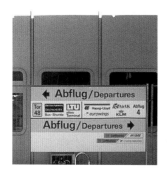
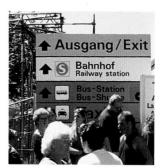

DÜSSELDORF AIRPORT
Signage system, 1996

The old signage (above) was extremely confusing and lacked any hierarchical structure. While reconstruction went on, makeshift towers (right) were put up to supply lots of information in one location. The new system (far right) avoids information overkill.

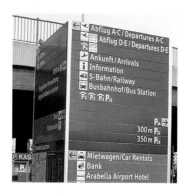
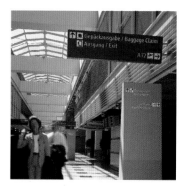

34

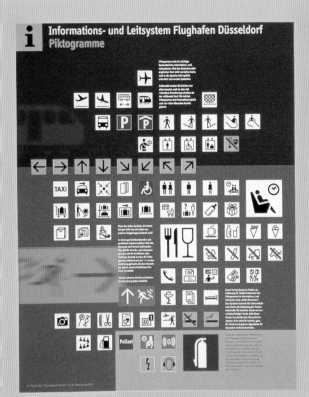

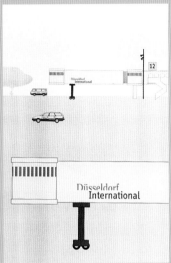

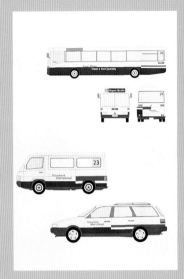

DÜSSELDORF AIRPORT
Signage system and corporate livery, from 1996

The pictograms used throughout the airport were based on those developed earlier by MetaDesign for the Berlin Transportation Authority. A structural hierarchy was developed for the new signage system. The success of MetaDesign's work led to a commission to design a corporate identity for the airport.

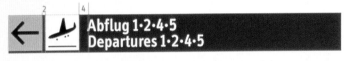

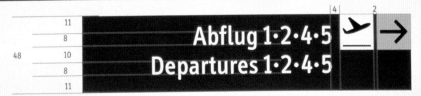

Zweizeiliger Text neben doppelt so großem Piktogramm. Das ist nur möglich , wenn die inhaltliche Aussage die gleiche ist (deutsch / englisch). Der Zeilenabstand wird verringert.
x-Höhe: 10 Units
Achtung: der Abstand vom Piktogramm zum Textbeträgt hier lediglich 4 Units!

Bei Platzmangel: zweizeiliger Text untereinander. Wenn die inhaltliche Aussage die gleiche ist (deutsch / englisch), wird der Zeilenabstand verringert.
x-Höhe: 8 Units

Abflug 1·2·4·5
Departures 1·2·4·5

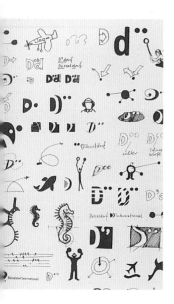

the most common routes that were taken by passengers. "Meanwhile, we had to work out how the signs would look and start to get some in place in the tents," says Schmidt. "There was no time for testing colors or experimenting with different typefaces and sizes. Nevertheless, we knew that our plan would need not only to solve the immediate problem, but also to serve the new airport when it opened."

A rich, dark green was chosen as the key color. "It provides really good contrast with white lettering, it is soft and calming, and no other German airports had adopted it," says Schmidt. The FF Info typeface, a design that Erik Spiekermann had been working on before the fire, proved to be invaluable in giving the new system character and clarity. Spiekermann's aim was to create an information system face that would be legible but also compact. FF Info takes up 12 percent less space than Univers or Helvetica, and is conceived to work well both in printed format and in illuminated signs.

"To get the signs in place as quickly as possible, we brought with us a manufacturer who could make signs on site, directly downloading the files from our computers. To speed things up still further, we even developed a software system that partly automated the design process. The pace was incredible: teams were working around the clock, and signs were installed as soon as they could be made," says Schmidt. MetaDesign's 3-D team worked on the design of the signage system's hardware; the modular system is extremely easy to assemble and has proved considerably cheaper than ready-made systems. Despite the six-week deadline, all 2,500 signs were completed and in place to provide clear way-finding through the vacation rush.

This was not the end of MetaDesign's involvement, however. "From the start of the project, it had been clear that the new way-finding system could only be the first step into a new identity," says Schmidt. "We were asked to develop a new logo, but instead turned around and asked them for a vision that the logo should express. Without that shared vision we would get stuck in a never-ending debate dominated by taste rather than strategy. We held a series of workshops, and the result was a strong platform upon which to develop the new identity."

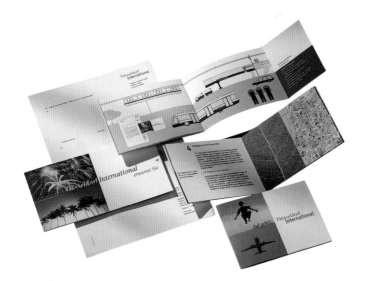

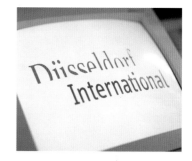

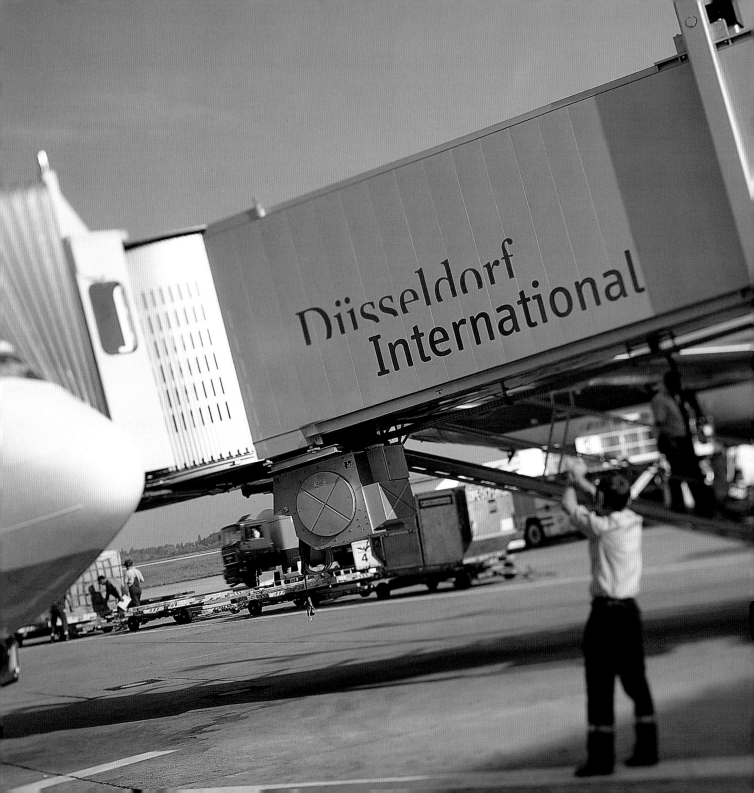

AFTER RAPID GROWTH in its stature as an authoritative voice in design commentary, it became clear that the British-based quarterly magazine *Graphics International* needed a facelift. "The high quality of the writing had rather overtaken the design, and the publication needed a new format in which it could really shine," explains project leader Tim Fendley of the London office. "The owners were planning a relaunch of the title as a monthly, and wanted to use that as an opportunity to relate the design to the content. Our brief was to give it more of a European feel."

The solution was to invest the design with a more formal appearance. "By doing this," says Fendley, "we were trying to reduce the design and almost make it invisible. We devised a system of hierarchies to support the text; this meant that headlines, standfirsts [subheadings], and boxed information didn't have to compete with the text for attention. The typefaces Minion and Myriad were chosen as the most appropriate, and they make a very clear read." A page grid was created that would allow maximum flexibility in the use of pictures. MetaDesign worked on the publication for 18 months through the period of transition to a new owner. The design is now handled in-house.

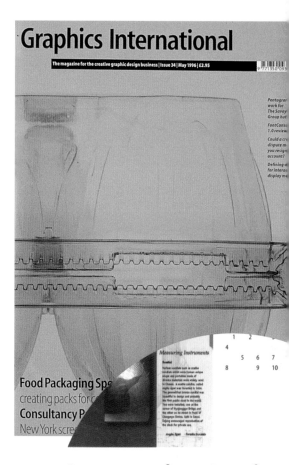

Food Packaging Sp
creating packs for
Consultancy P
New York scre

Innovative Design

As companies take the contributio their business more seriously, will lead of Samsung and take the train designers in-house, asks Josef De

↓

The relationship between design education and the design industry has always been good, if complex. In Europe and the US, professiona designers have far greater involve- ent with the education of future of designers than i

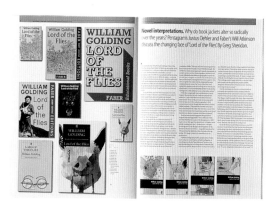

GRAPHICS
INTERNATIONAL
Magazine redesign, 1996

**MetaDesign's new-look spreads
are ordered and rational, but allow
for plenty of visual flexibility.**

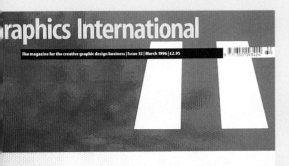

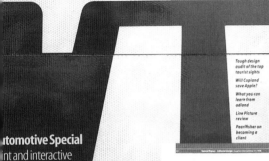

GRAPHICS INTERNATIONAL
Magazine redesign, 1996

The magazine covers look fresh and inviting, while the inside page design gives imagery plenty of impact. The detail at left below shows the treatment of main text, standfirsts [subheadings], headings, and picture captions.

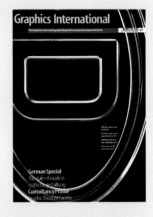

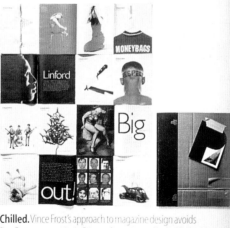

Chilled. Vince Frost's approach to magazine design avoids Ray Gun-esque antics in favour of restraint and logic. Michael Evamy talks to the designer behind The Independent Magazine, Big, and the new D&AD Newsletter.

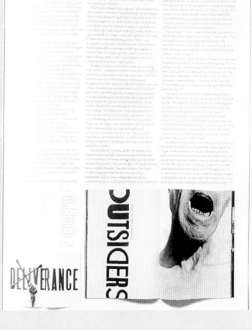

Springer

AFTER A SERIES of management changes, the leading German scientific book publisher Springer decided to take the unusual step of announcing its relaunch through design. To mark a new era for the company, its books and journals were to be given a facelift. "When we first met the client, we asked if they had a corporate design, and they all nodded very positively. But then we pointed out that since all their business cards looked completely different, their design didn't seem to be working," explains MetaDesign partner Pia Betton of the Berlin office.

The brief was to modernize and invigorate the book jackets and Springer brand while revising the logo, or creating a replacement for it, at the same time. "We started by considering the logo and decided to leave it alone. It is very well known to Springer's audience and therefore has considerable brand equity. In fact, the logo provided the key to our design strategy. Springer means 'knight' in German, and it is the horse's head of the knight chess-piece that is prominent in the logo. We also learned that the company's founder was a fanatical chess player, so we developed a design based on the graphic of the knight's move on a chessboard: two moves up and one diagonally, like an L-shape with the corner missing."

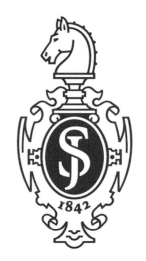

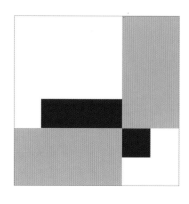

SPRINGER
Corporate design, 1991

As part of its revamp of Springer's image, MetaDesign redrew the company logo and devised a system of book covers based on the 3:2 move of a chessboard knight. The other elements of the system include a color matrix, pictorial style, and typographic specification.

SPRINGER
Corporate design, from 1991

The new corporate look makes an impact at the 1996 Frankfurt Book Fair.

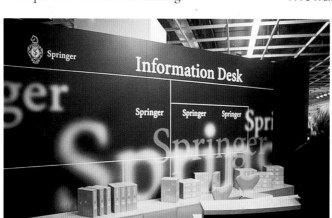

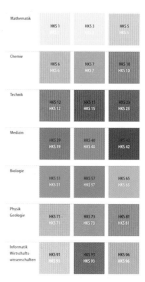

40

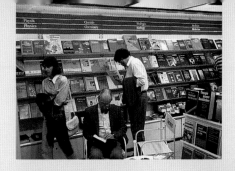

This simple but effective device is deployed up to three times on each book's cover, used in different sizes and interpretations. Sometimes it takes the form of solid blocks of color, while at others it may appear as a soft tint, as a frame for photographic imagery, or as a sequence of dots. At times it is so subtle as to be almost subliminal, but it is always unmistakable. The Springer logo appears on both the front cover and the spine, where it is featured in the same position on books of all sizes to give instant shelf recognition. To further boost brand impact and increase consistency in the jacket designs, a restricted palette of colors was created. This comprises seven colors, each in "warm" and "cool" versions. The three main areas of specialism were color-coded: mathematical books are given a yellow theme, biological books a blue theme, and medical books, green.

MetaDesign also worked on restructuring the interiors of the books and devised strong templates into which imagery and text could be placed. A new typeface, Springer Minion, was created to improve the clarity of these often text-heavy volumes.

"After we had established the principles of the design, we worked on the first sequence of books to be published," explains Betton. "However, because Springer has a backlist of some 20,000 volumes and issues a further 1,800 or so every year, we knew we could not take on the job full time. Instead we created a small design manual and handed the work back to the in-house production department. The transition was straightforward, and we've been delighted to see how the in-house team has really pushed the concept by coming up with really exciting variations and interpretations of the theme."

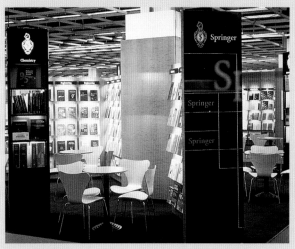

SPRINGER
Corporate design, 1991

The former book-fair stand (top) served to confirm the stereotype that scientific books are dull and worthy, whereas the new stand epitomizes the new, fresh-thinking attitude. Meta's analysis of the publishing program led to a streamlining of the production process and the scrapping of several outmoded formats.

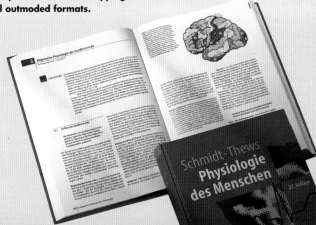

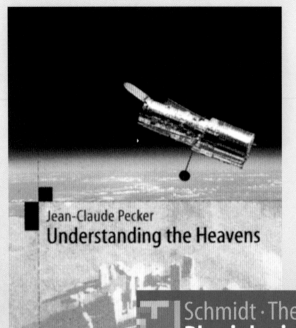

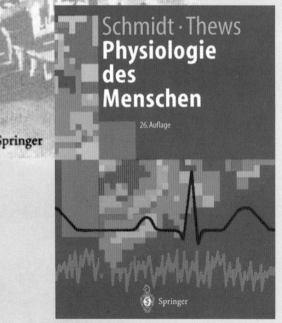

SPRINGER
Cover designs, 1994

The former designs, right, lacked any sort of family homogeneity and created visual disharmony. All covers are now based on interpretations of the L-shaped geometric grid at large and small scales. No matter what size the book, a sense of order is created on the shelf by locating the logo in the same position on each spine.

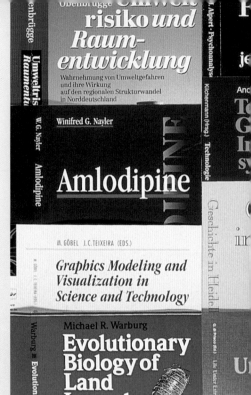

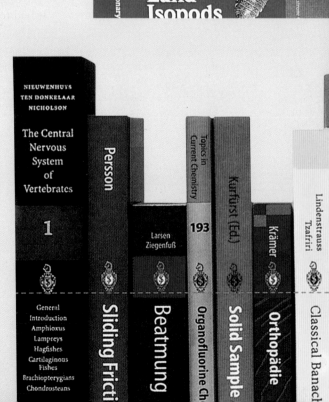

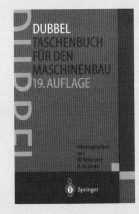

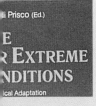

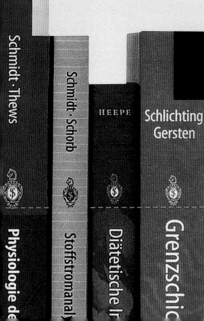

SPRINGER
Cover designs, 1994

After an initial handing-over period, Springer's in-house design team began producing books to MetaDesign's guidelines. The L-shaped device can be interpreted in an almost infinite variety of ways.

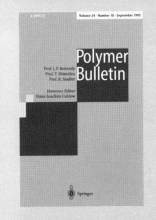

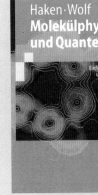

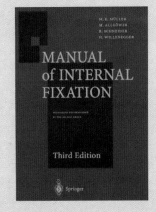

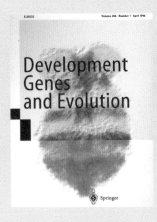

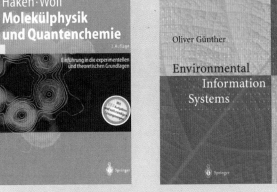

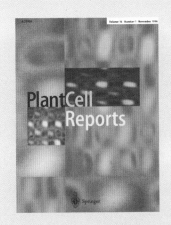

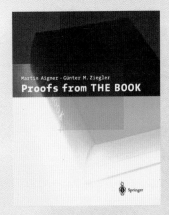

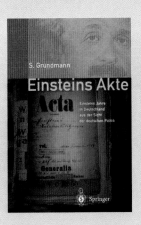

Artranspennine98

F THE SUDDEN APPEARANCE OF A
20-foot (6-meter)-high, yellow lamb stand-
ing in the English landscape raised a few
eyebrows, the fact that it had an enormous banana
attached to its side was too much for some to
contemplate. But this Taro Chiezo sculpture,
Super Lamb Banana, was symbolic of the ambi-
tions of the massive international art exhibition
staged across the Pennine region during 1998.
One of the central aims of the exhibition was
to remove art from its usual gallery setting and
deliver it into the community: to libraries, parks,
markets, hotels, and the street. "It was clear from
the start that this project was going to be adventurous," says Frances Jackson of MetaDesign
London, who completed the identity and sign
system with Sam Davy and Gail Mellows.

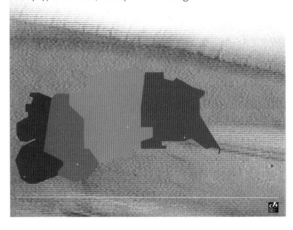

artranspennine98
an exhibition of international
contemporary visual art

23 may – 16 august
a new kind of exhibition: 50 artists, 40 artworks,
30 sites across the pennines revealing the life,
culture and diversity of the region.

for more information call: 0845 30 98989
http://www.artranspennine.org.uk

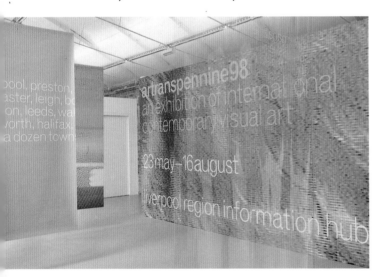

ARTRANSPENNINE98
Poster, folder, and interior of Liverpool exhibition, 1998

**MetaDesign's comprehensive design program for
the UK's largest-ever art show included exhibition
design, posters, a Web site, signs, guides, and
catalogs. The logo, seen in the poster top right, was
based on the geographical area hosting the art event.**

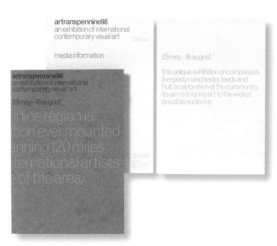

44

The joint organizers—the Tate Gallery Liverpool and the Henry Moore Institute in Leeds—originally came to MetaDesign to commission maps to guide visitors around the 30 venues and events. These were spread from the west to east coasts, taking in Liverpool, Leeds, Manchester, and Hull. More than 60 artists were involved in 40 projects. "After a brainstorming session, it became clear that maps were only part of the solution to moving people around the area. We came out of that meeting with the brief to create an identity and all the printed material and signs, together with additional items such as the Web site."

After an exploratory trip around the region armed with a video camera, the designers devised an identity based on a symbolic map of the area. This was divided into solid segments (colored purple, orange, red, and burgundy), a sequence of grainy images taken from their video footage, and typography. The face used was Monotype Grotesque 215. In the weeks preceding the summertime show, MetaDesign produced dozens of items of publicity, marketing, and information material. The work has since continued with the compilation of a book to commemorate the event.

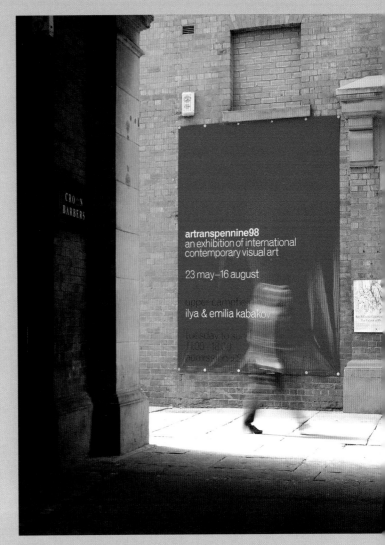

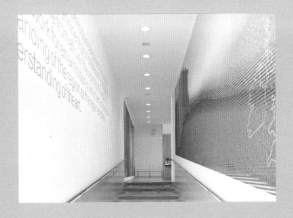

ARTRANSPENNINE98
Banner, Manchester, and interior of Leeds exhibition, 1998

A simple banner demonstrates the power and clarity of good information design. The strong typography was an instantly recognizable element of the identity, as seen in the entrance to one of the exhibition venues in Leeds.

45

Getty Center

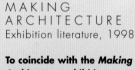

MAKING AN EXHIBITION about the building of the new Getty Center in Los Angeles sounded like an intriguing challenge. But MetaDesign's San Francisco designers realized the full scale of the task only when it was discovered that they first had to trawl through a warehouse full of plans, detailed drawings, documents, letters, material samples, models, and assorted artifacts. "The center is designed by Richard Meier and took 14 years to build; this was the entire archive of the construction process and the people involved," explains project leader Terry Irwin. "We didn't have a reputation as exhibition designers, but were approached for the job as information designers; our task in the first instance was to manage and edit the material. We then had to devise a way of telling the story in both an interesting and an engaging way to an audience made up of people who were not familiar with the building process."

MAKING
ARCHITECTURE
Exhibition literature, 1998

To coincide with the *Making Architecture* exhibition, MetaDesign created a walking guide to the Getty Center. Right: center spread; opposite: cover and intro panels.

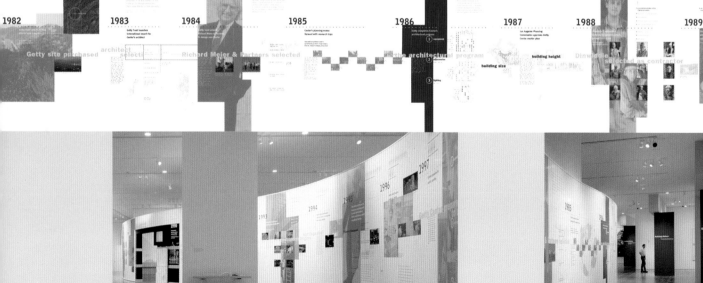

The key to imposing order on the vast archive was a curving wall. "This provided our timeline, and formed the center of the exhibition. At 100 feet [30 meters] long and 15 feet [5 meters] tall, it provided a vertical surface for displaying images and documents, and also gave us three-dimensional possibilities: we could display models, materials, and video interviews by setting display cases and monitors into the wall." Entitled *Making Architecture*, the exhibition opened in 1998.

The visual material was supported by a text. "Through our use of typography we have been able to build options for how the visitor views the show. There's a hierarchy of ordering, which means that if you want to assimilate the story quickly it's possible to pick up the basic idea in about ten minutes. But if you're interested in the detail and want to read everything, it'll take 45 minutes." MetaDesign also produced literature to accompany the exhibition.

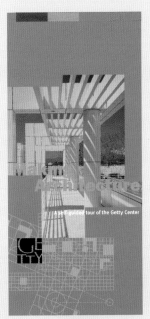

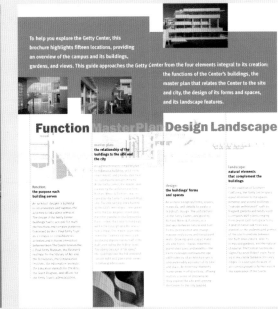

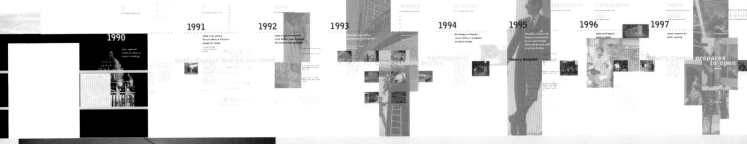

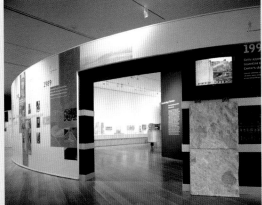

MAKING
ARCHITECTURE
Exhibition, Getty Center, 1998

The exhibition was based on an informative timeline that chronicled the 14-year process of building the Getty Center.

47

IDEO

HEN GLOBAL product design company IDEO decided to launch a Web site, it knew this was a job for someone else. "One of the most difficult tasks for designers is to design for themselves," confirms Rick Lowe, co-creative director of MetaDesign San Francisco. "Because IDEO wanted to secure its Web presence as rapidly as possible, the initial brief was to design an interim site. The immediate need was to build a site that would operate as a marketing tool and which would guide prospective clients toward the nearest of the group's eight offices worldwide."

Bearing in mind that the site would be expanded in stages, Meta conceived the first set of designs as a framework into which further information could be slotted at a later date. "We went for lots of width and little depth," explains Lowe. "The idea was that potential customers visiting the site would make quick hits to take a look at the vast range of products that IDEO works on, and then be able to locate and talk to the appropriate person. For the more engaged visitor there would be a greater opportunity to linger on the site and explore in depth the details and story of each product."

IDEO was also very keen that to create maximum interest in the site, it had to be technically innovative and possess what David Kelly, CEO of IDEO, described as the "wow factor." The designers rose to the challenge and built in unusual features such as the automatic horizontal scrolling and a bevy of Flash animations. Since its introduction, and to the delight of David Kelly, the site has won numerous awards and has had exceptional recognition from the design and business communities. Work is now in progress on the next phase to expand the site.

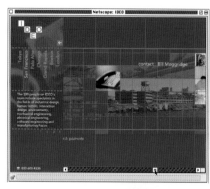

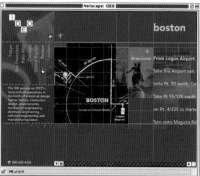

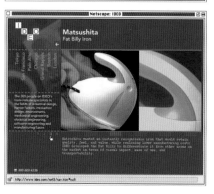

IDEO
Web site, 1998

Screens from the IDEO Web site developed by MetaDesign San Francisco. Borrowing imagery from a designer's sketchbook and technical drawing manuals, the site explores the nature of design.

IDEO
Web site, 1998

Technically sophisticated, the site is an opportunity for IDEO to showcase some of the many products it designs for clients worldwide. Flash animations and Javascript programming automate a long panorama of product shots, housed within a grid framework. An animated intro screen (below) allows time for the images in the main site to load.

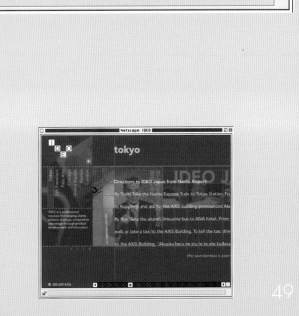

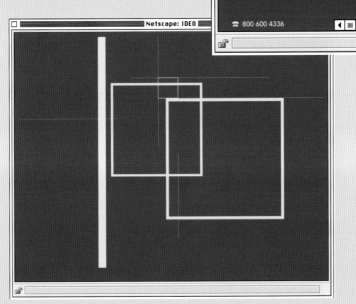

Nike

WITH A REPUTATION for creating some of the world's most exciting retail environments, sportswear manufacturers Nike called in MetaDesign San Francisco to work on the graphics for a new series of shops. "Our starting point was Nike's vast and impressive collection of sports photography; they've worked with some of the very best photographers and have really powerful images of the world's greatest athletes," says Rick Lowe, creative co-director of the project. "There was a story that needed to be told."

The 80,000-square-foot (7,400-square-meter) store in Honolulu was the prototype. MetaDesign San Francisco developed an entire system of graphic items, ranging from displays showcasing Nike products to massive 10 × 20-foot (3 × 6-meter) photographic images, complete with story boxes about the lives and most famous moments of different athletes. Engraved commemorative plaques were set into the floor to celebrate sporting personalities and achievements. MetaDesign also developed a store directory and display signs to differentiate the sports categories. "We wanted to make these dynamic photo-narratives express the action and emotion of sport. The environment is a celebration of athletic ability and product innovation that creates an emotional connection that inspires consumers to participate in sports." Following the opening in Honolulu, further stores in Toronto and Melbourne have been produced by Nike's in-house design teams, based on the MetaDesign concept, and a German-American team worked together on the spring 1999 opening of NikeTown Berlin.

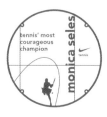

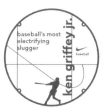

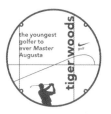

NIKETOWN
Store graphics, 1998

The interior detailing includes a series of metal alloy plaques, sunk into the floor, that celebrate great sporting characters.

NIKETOWN
Packaging, 1998

Shopping bags and gift boxes were devised by MetaDesign San Francisco for the Toronto and Melbourne stores.

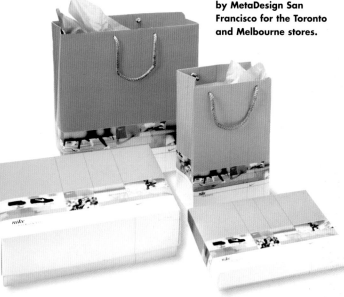

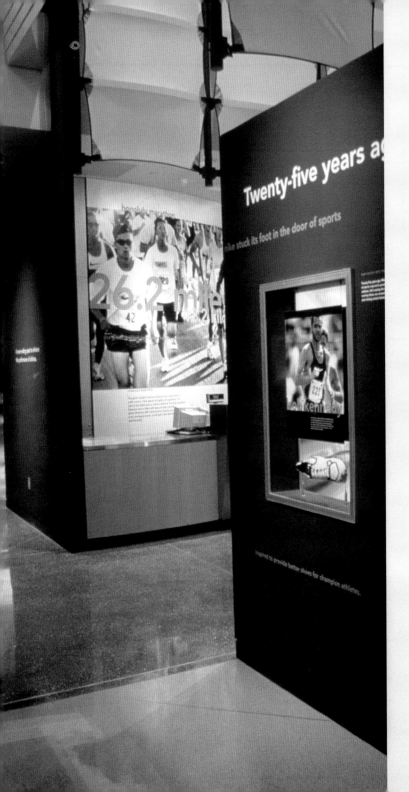

Twenty-five years ag

Nike stuck its foot in the door of sports

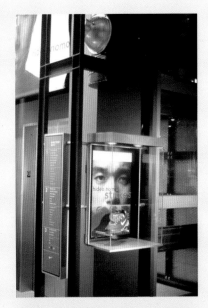

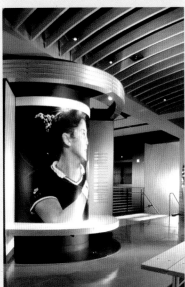

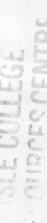

NIKETOWN
Store interiors, 1998

More than mere retail outlets, the NikeTown stores resemble shrines to modern sporting heroes and celebrate the role of Nike products in the pursuit of excellence.

THE ENGLISH LANGUAGE provided the inspiration for the new typeface devised by Meta to mark Glasgow's celebratory year as the UK City of Architecture and Design. The Berlin and London offices joined forces for the task: Erik Spiekermann and Ole Schäfer worked on the face in Germany, while the London office constructed the identity system and implementation package. The commission was won in an international competition staged by the event organizer late in 1996. The brief was to develop a face that would be "distinctive and memorable, reflect the spirit of a contemporary city of architecture and design, and help promote Glasgow worldwide."

"I started with the concept of language and how to express it through type," explains Spiekermann. "The face was a response to how Glaswegians use language and how it sounds. It had to be strong and punchy, even guttural. I also wanted to illustrate some of the peculiarities of the written language—for example, the word 'read' can be pronounced in two different ways, so I wanted to be able to write it in two different ways."

The resulting well-built, muscular typeface uses under- and overlining for vowels as well as a set of ligatures for consonant combinations (such as "ch") and for the ten most commonly used words in the English language (such as "he," "of," "and," "it," "for," and "in"). These visual devices combine to reinforce the strength of the face and add the idea (appropriate to the festival's theme) of being able to "construct" the language. Spiekermann's pencil-sketch concepts were developed and digitized by Schäfer.

Meanwhile, in England, work was underway to give the face a context. "We built a design system that was passed on to Scottish

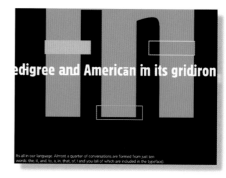

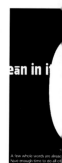

dddodoDeéeEfffFgḡgoGhhHH

ndKll!lLmmMMnññnNooōoOpp̄

sssStttTuuUvvVwwwWxxX

!22th@33£ffl44$fi55%ffi

8st*99ḡ(00ono).,/¿?'»«""\

eŒõéí!○!©*←→↑←↙↘

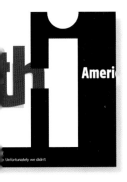

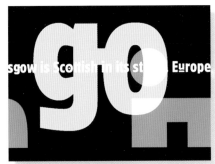

America...sgow is Scottish in its st... Europe

...n. Unfortunately we didn't

GLASGOW 1999
Typeface design, 1998

The Glasgow 1999 face looks complex
because of its many variants, but the
design rules are simple and nonrestrictive.
A type "movie" (left), showing creative uses
of the typeface, was put together to inspire
Scottish designers and promote the event.

Like the typeface, the design guidelines and all literature connected with the year-long festival were intended to be as flexible as possible. A vigorous graphic pattern is created by the exploitation of large type.

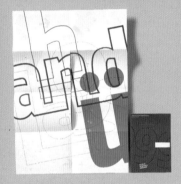

design studios so they could create posters, exhibition catalogs, and other visual material relating to the year-long event," explains Tim Fendley of the London office. "The identity comprises the family of fonts; graphic elements, and a 12-color palette. In line with the layout of Glasgow's streets, a 9.99° angle was used as a layout technique." The typeface consists of three fonts: one containing numerous linking characters, ligatures, and accents; a conventional character set; and a third font which comprises a variety of dingbats and ten versions of each of the two parts of the logo, giving a total of 99 different combinations. Included with the CD of the fonts is an inspirational type movie showing creative uses of the typeface.

"Knowing that designers will want to experiment as much as possible, we built in plenty of flexibility," says Fendley. "Our guidelines were deliberately permissive and are based on the themes of construction, flexibility, and contrast." This was presented in the typeface and design resource manuals, which are supplied with a CD-ROM of fonts and templates.

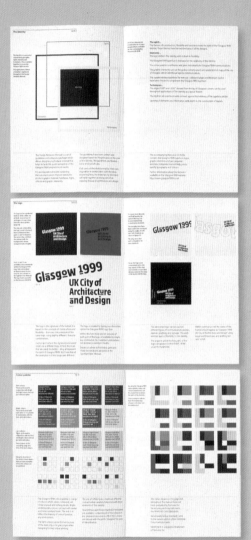

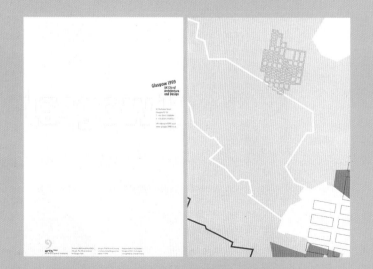

The literature has variety but maintains a coherent and instantly recognizable brand image. The devices of type mixed with a graphic depiction of the city areas and grid make for exciting stationery.

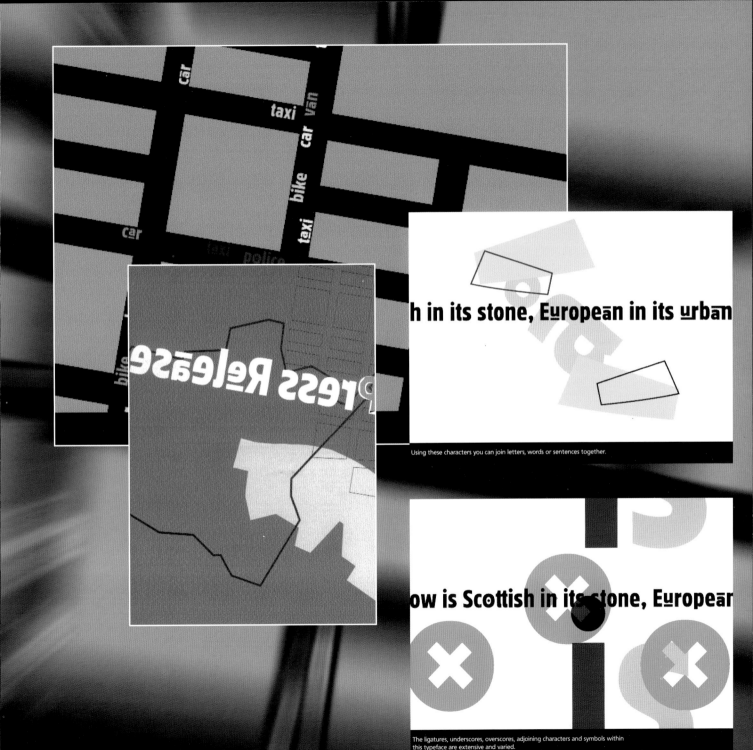

car

taxi vān

car

bike

car

taxi

taxi

police

bike

ress Release

h in its stone, European in its urban

Using these characters you can join letters, words or sentences together.

ow is Scottish in its stone, European

The ligatures, underscores, overscores, adjoining characters and symbols within
this typeface are extensive and varied.

Barclays Global Investors

THE FINANCIAL MARKET has not normally been noted for its adventurous forays in design, but when Barclays Global Investors (BGI) came to MetaDesign the company asked for the unusual. The brief was enigmatic: "The client said they had Pears Soap, but what they wanted was the Pirelli calendar," says managing director Robin Richmond of the London office.

BGI was a new brand, born out of Barclays' purchase of the investment bank Wells Fargo Nikko. MetaDesign San Francisco had been called in for the corporate identity redesign. In Europe, meanwhile, BGI wanted to broaden its theater of operations. MetaDesign's London office was asked to help. "The new company was putting together some innovative products and wanted to shout about them. Having seen the trend in British national banks toward using design imaginatively as a powerful communication tool, BGI was prepared to break City (of London) ranks and produce visually exciting material." The set of a dozen brochures is fresh and clean in its design, and particularly noteworthy for its striking photographic imagery. "The metaphor of growth was a central theme, so each brochure features detailed pictures of leaves, flowers, or trees. The hyper-real style was set by photographer Toby McFarlan Pond." In an arena of unexciting literature, the BGI brochures not only firmly established the bank's new brand image, but also created a striking and memorable marketing campaign.

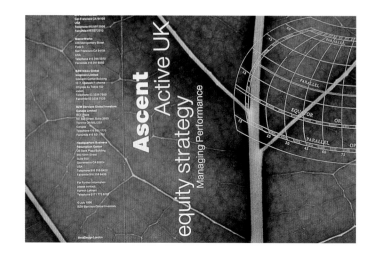

BARCLAYS GLOBAL INVESTORS
Marketing literature, 1997

MetaDesign studios in London and San Francisco worked jointly to devise a refreshingly unstuffy corporate image. Projects have included marketing brochures, newsletters, interactive presentations, and templates for internal communications.

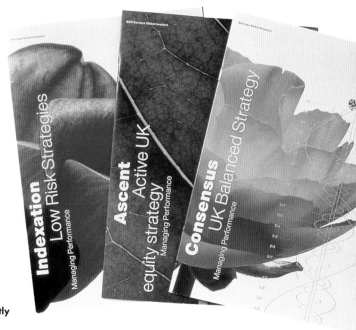

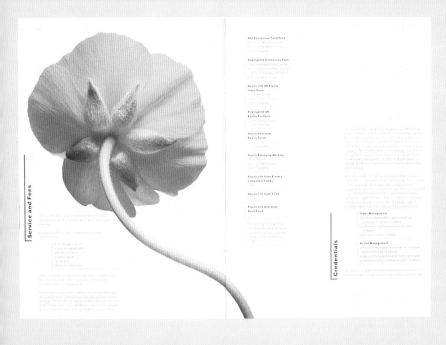

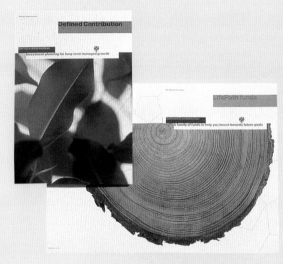

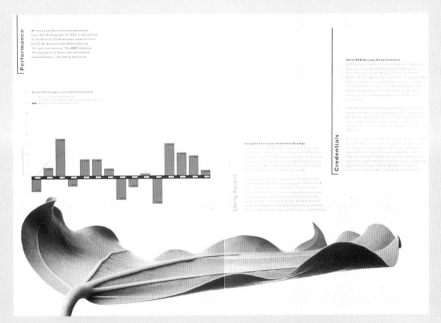

BARCLAYS GLOBAL
INVESTORS
Marketing literature, 1997

**Attention to typographic detail
is complemented by stunning
photography. The result is a
series of memorable brochures
that stand out from the usual
safe-but-dull financial literature.**

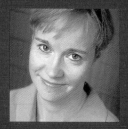

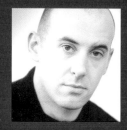

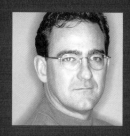

Pia Betton

Pia Betton (MetaDesign Berlin) is responsible for human resources and project development. Born in Copenhagen, she formerly worked for Eleven Danes Design, one of the most renowned Scandinavian design groups. Her career has also encompassed typesetting and advertising. She has worked at MetaDesign Berlin since 1991, heading the design team developing international corporate design for Audi.

Tim Fendley

Tim Fendley (MetaDesign London) has developed numerous international projects in Europe and the U.S. In 1991 he set up Union Design with Robin Richmond and in 1995 became a founding partner in MetaDesign London. Fendley is a visiting lecturer at the Computer Related Design masters program at the Royal College of Art, London, and has lectured widely on design.

Bill Hill

Bill Hill (MetaDesign San Francisco) formerly worked with IDEO Product Development, where he designed and directed projects for firms such as Hewlett-Packard, Adobe, and Apple Computer. He cofounded MetaDesign San Francisco in 1992 with Terry Irwin. In addition to management and business development responsibilites at MetaDesign, Hill focuses on human-centered issues and raising design awareness.

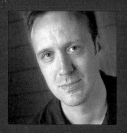

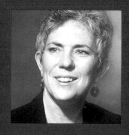

Charly Frech

Charly Frech (MetaDesign Berlin) supervises MetaDesign Berlin's Internet team and software design and technology group. His postgraduate thesis concerned the man/machine interface and the computer as a tool for communication and work. In 1992 he founded MetaLog, a subsidiary specializing in multimedia applications and design management software (incorporated into MetaDesign in 1994). Today he is responsible for innovation in the whole company.

Terry Irwin

Terry Irwin (MetaDesign San Francisco) took her masters degree at the Basel School of Design, Switzerland. Formerly a project director at Landor Associates, she cofounded MetaDesign San Francisco in 1992 with Bill Hill. Irwin has taught classes in typography, color theory, and graphic design, and is currently an adjunct professor at California College of Arts and Crafts in San Francisco.

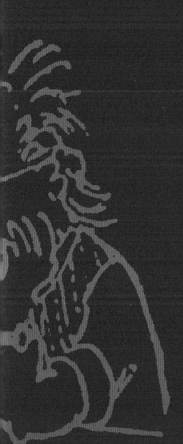

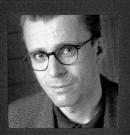

Hans Christian Krüger

Hans Christian Krüger (MetaDesign Berlin) is one of the founding partners of MetaDesign phase III and oversees all financial activities in the Meta group. His background is in business administration and banking. Since joining MetaDesign in 1990, he has overseen the acquisition of the prepress company CitySatz and the founding of MetaDesign San Francisco and London.

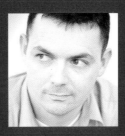

Robin Richmond

Robin Richmond (MetaDesign London) trained and practiced as a graphic designer in London and Toronto. In 1995 he became a founding partner in MetaDesign London. Since 1998 he has been responsible for new business development, human resources, and the management of day-to-day operations. He is a founding member of the committee for the M.A. in Typographic Studies at the London College of Printing.

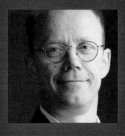

Erik Spiekermann

Erik Spiekermann (MetaDesign Berlin) cofounded MetaDesign phase III in 1990 with Uli Mayer and Hans Christian Krüger. Spiekermann designs information systems and typefaces. He travels among the three offices, lecturing and presenting MetaDesign on the way. He is vice president of the German Design Council, president of the International Institute for Information Design, and Professor for Communication Design at Bremen University.

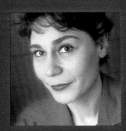

Uli Mayer

Uli Mayer (MetaDesign Berlin) cofounded MetaDesign phase III in 1990. She is currently working on new approaches to corporate design processes, developing tools and techniques for large-scale identity projects. She formerly worked for the Berlin design firm FAB Kommunikation, and holds a teaching post at the European School of Management.

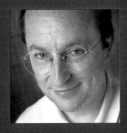

Bruno Schmidt

Bruno Schmidt (MetaDesign Berlin) is responsible for new business and corporate communication at MetaDesign. He formerly worked in advertising and teaching, and became a client of MetaDesign Berlin while working on advertising strategies for German schoolbook publisher Cornelsen. He joined MetaDesign in 1992, where he initially managed the Berlin transportation project and later founded the Audi corporate design team.

Chronology

1947
Erik Spiekermann born in Stadthagen, West Germany.

1967
Spiekermann enrolls at Berlin's Free University to study art history and English.

1973
Moves to London. Teaches at the London College of Printing and works as a freelance designer and typographer for clients in London and Berlin.

1979
Founds MetaDesign with Dieter Heil (based in London) and Florian Fischer (based in Berlin). In 1983 the three partners decide on an amicable split; MetaDesign GmbH ceases operations, but the name remains registered.

1984
The German post office invites bids for a large corporate design account. Spiekermann enters as MetaDesign, helped by Dieter Heil (now at Sedley Place Design, London). They win the account. Sedley Place buys Spiekermann's and Fischer's shares in MetaDesign, takes over the post office account, and forms Sedley Place Berlin. Spiekermann works as a consultant on the project (until 1987). In late 1984 Spiekermann sets up MetaDesign phase II; clients include Berthold AG, Scangraphic, and Linotype.

1990
Opening of MetaDesign phase III. Spiekermann with new partners Uli Mayer (designer) and Hans Christian Krüger (financial director), together with seven designers, start in a new office in Potsdamer Platz. The company grows to 15 people by the middle of the year, and moves into larger offices. Clients include Berlin Transportation Authority, Herman Miller, and Agfa.

1991
New clients include GrundKreditBank, Philip Morris (Marlboro Design Shop), Einstein Café, and Europäischer Filmpreis (European Film Award). MetaDesign wins German Design Award for customer information for the Berlin Transportation Authority.

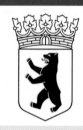

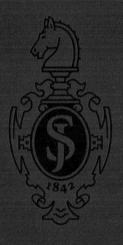

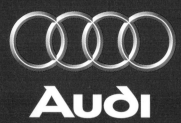

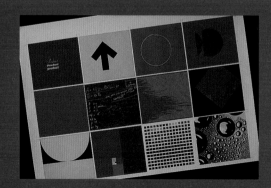

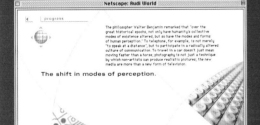

Stop Stealing Sheep
& find out how type works

Erik Spiekermann
& E.M. Ginger

- ---> Type is everywhere
- ---> What is type?
- ---> Looking at type
- ---> Type with a purpose
- ---> Type builds character
- ---> Types of type
- ---> How it works
- ---> Putting it to work
- ---> There is no bad type

friendfactory
we're all connected

1992

Berlin office grows to 30 people. Founding of MetaLog for the development of multimedia systems; an early project is the interactive information system for the Jewish Museum, Frankfurt. MetaDesign San Francisco opens, with partners Terry Irwin and Bill Hill together with six employees. New clients include Hewlett-Packard, VISA USA, Adobe, and Apple Computer.

1993

Further growth in Berlin and San Francisco offices. Berlin takes on increasing numbers of corporate identity and corporate design projects. New clients include Springer publishers, Berlin local government (Berlin); 3DO, Sun Microsystems (San Francisco).

1994

New clients include TV and radio station Westdeutscher Rundfunk, Boehringer Ingelheim, Willy Brandt Haus (Berlin); VizAbility, Wells Fargo Nikko, Levi Strauss & Co (San Francisco). MetaDesign wins Beacon Award for Berlin Transport System identity.

1995

Berlin office implements new decentralized structure and becomes international corporate design lead agency for Audi and VW. New San Francisco clients include Ernst & Young LLP, Texas Instruments, and IBM. London office opens in August with partners Tim Fendley and Robin Richmond and a staff of four. Clients include Tangerine and VCG.

1996

Pia Betton, Charly Frech, and Bruno Schmidt become partners in the Berlin office. New clients include architecture publishers Bauwelt, Düsseldorf airport (Berlin); J. Paul Getty Trust, Scudder, Tandem, *MacUser* (San Francisco); Union Bank of Switzerland, *Graphics International* (London).

1997

MetaDesign Berlin becomes Germany's largest design company, with 150 staff. New clients include Bosch, Hewi fittings, Viag Interkom telecommunications, German Federal Goverment (Berlin); Sony, AT&T, Netscape, IDEO (San Francisco); Barclays Global Investors (London).

1998

New clients include Heidelberg, Koch Dureco Group, Peace Works (Berlin); Nike, Fuse (San Francisco); Glasgow 1999, Artranspennine98, Skoda (London). New premises for MetaDesign Berlin are found, move planned for late 1999.

1999

New clients include Deutsche Bahn Cargo, Robert-Koch-Institut (Berlin). San Francisco grows to 50 employees, London to 27.

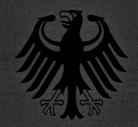

61

Index

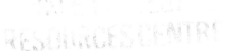

Acknowledgments

The publishers wish to thank all at MetaDesign Berlin, San Francisco, and London for their kind assistance with all aspects of this book.

Picture credits
Rainer Christoph: 28 bottom, 31 background.
Deffner & Schormann: pages 11 top left, 31 top.
Philip Götz: page 33 all, 41 bottom.
Stephan Klonk: page 22 bottom left.
Yorck Maecke: pages 22 top right, 25 top right.
Stefan Schilling: pages 34 bottom middle and right, 36 right, 37.
Tilman Schwarz: page 14.
Erik Weiß: page 10 bottom left.

All images courtesy MetaDesign, apart from page 38 top left and right (courtesy Graphics International).

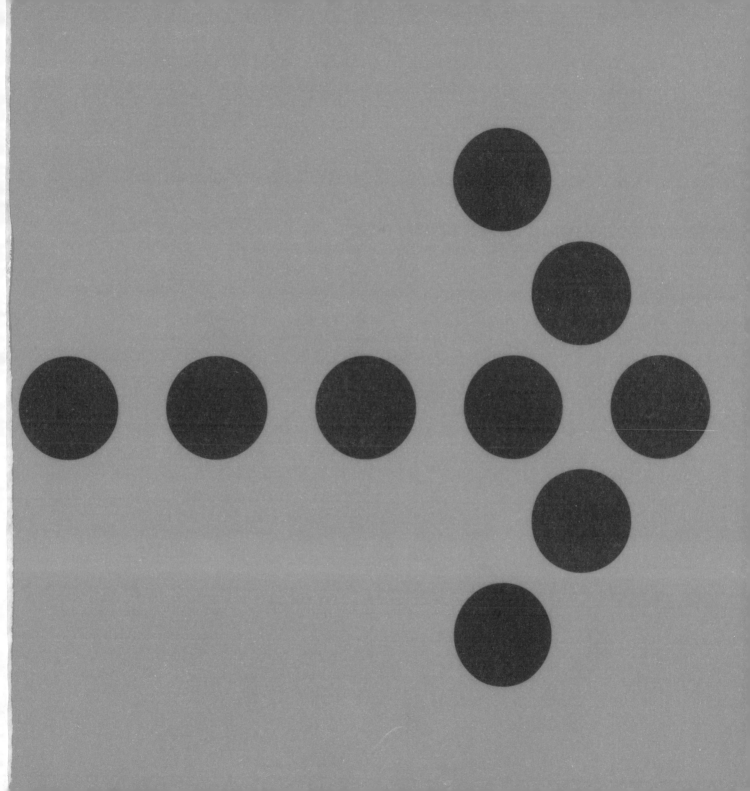

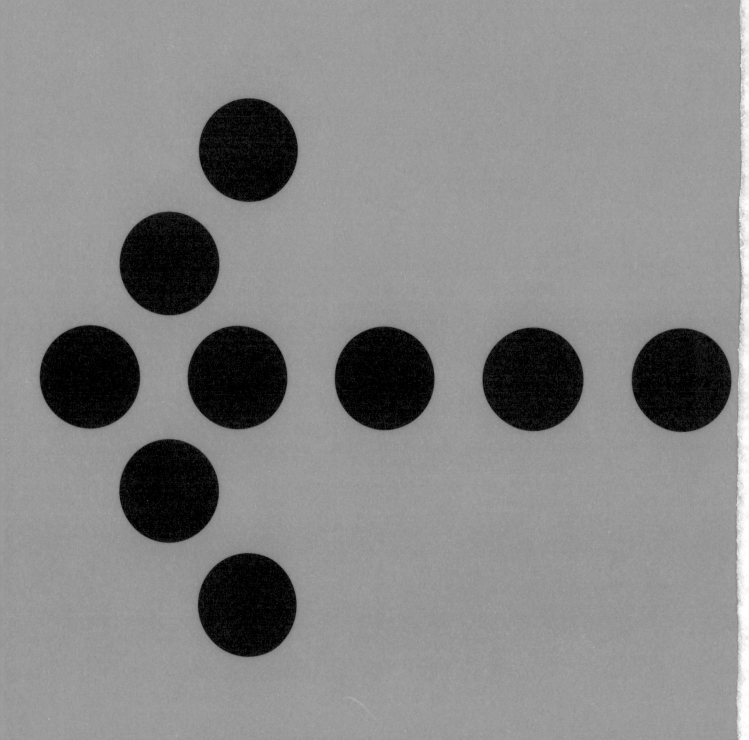